Waves of Hope

'An extraordinary book. Authentic, intimate and often uplifting first-person accounts of the experience of severe mental illness and the therapeutic power of ECT. The stories pull no punches and should be read by everyone who wants to understand why we still need ECT and what it means to have the treatment.'

Professor Robert Howard, University College London

'*Waves of Hope: Personal Stories of ECT* debunks the misunderstanding and stigma surrounding ECT, and, best of all, does it in patients' own words. Their stories are heartbreaking, but also heartening, as they chronicle paths to recovery, ultimately facilitated by ECT. Kudos to these patients and their families for the courage to speak out, and to Professor Kirov for bringing them together. This well-curated collection of highly personal vignettes is a must-read for anyone who wants to learn the reality about a venerable treatment that remains a vital, often life-saving, part of modern psychiatric medicine. This book definitively answers the question, "Do they still do that?" with a resounding "Yes, we still do that, and these stories explain why."'

Charles H. Kellner, MD, Professor Emeritus of Psychiatry and Behavioral Sciences, Medical University of South Carolina

'In this invaluable book, George Kirov does a remarkable job of bridging the gap between clinical knowledge and real-world lived experience. Each chapter, written by an expert with personal experience, offers the reader unique insights beyond the psychiatrist's perspective. It provides an intimate look at what patients go through and how distressing side effects fuel anxiety. The goal, according to Kirov, is "to lift the mystery". But this book does much more – it tackles the stigma surrounding ECT by allowing readers to meet people with personal experience and hear their stories, each one worth telling and sharing.'

Pascal Sienaert, Professor of Psychiatry and Lead Psychiatrist for the Academic Centre for ECT and Neuromodulation, University Psychiatric Centre KU Leuven in Belgium; Chair of the European Forum for ECT; Associate Editor of the *Journal of ECT*

Waves of Hope

Personal Stories of ECT

Edited by

George Kirov
Cardiff University

Shaftesbury Road, Cambridge CB2 8EA, United Kingdom

One Liberty Plaza, 20th Floor, New York, NY 10006, USA

477 Williamstown Road, Port Melbourne, VIC 3207, Australia

314–321, 3rd Floor, Plot 3, Splendor Forum, Jasola District Centre, New Delhi – 110025, India

103 Penang Road, #05–06/07, Visioncrest Commercial, Singapore 238467

Cambridge University Press is part of Cambridge University Press & Assessment, a department of the University of Cambridge.

We share the University's mission to contribute to society through the pursuit of education, learning and research at the highest international levels of excellence.

www.cambridge.org
Information on this title: www.cambridge.org/9781009554619

DOI: 10.1017/9781009554572

© The Royal College of Psychiatrists 2025

This publication is in copyright. Subject to statutory exception and to the provisions of relevant collective licensing agreements, no reproduction of any part may take place without the written permission of Cambridge University Press & Assessment.

When citing this work, please include a reference to the DOI 10.1017/9781009554572

First published 2025

A catalogue record for this publication is available from the British Library

A Cataloging-in-Publication data record for this book is available from the Library of Congress

ISBN 978-1-009-55461-9 Paperback

Cambridge University Press & Assessment has no responsibility for the persistence or accuracy of URLs for external or third-party internet websites referred to in this publication and does not guarantee that any content on such websites is, or will remain, accurate or appropriate.

Every effort has been made in preparing this book to provide accurate and up-to-date information that is in accord with accepted standards and practice at the time of publication. Although case histories are drawn from actual cases, every effort has been made to disguise the identities of the individuals involved. Nevertheless, the authors, editors, and publishers can make no warranties that the information contained herein is totally free from error, not least because clinical standards are constantly changing through research and regulation. The authors, editors, and publishers therefore disclaim all liability for direct or consequential damages resulting from the use of material contained in this book. Readers are strongly advised to pay careful attention to information provided by the manufacturer of any drugs or equipment that they plan to use.

Illustrations: Milton Cordoba

Developmental editing: Jennifer Gilroy

Proofreading: Ruth Roberts

Coming up with a cover image for the book took some time. We considered many options until one idea immediately received everybody's approval. We decided to use the image for Jan's chapter, redrawn in colour. It depicts Jan with her three children, standing on the veranda of a hotel in Nice, enjoying the sunset and relaxing after the tumultuous events described in her story. Jan had requested this image because her children were the most important people in her life and because their stories related closely to the events described in the chapter, such as the postnatal psychosis she had experienced. Our illustrator, Milton, took the job seriously and explained the details: *'Darkness is portrayed in the silhouettes of the people. The variety of people of different ages and genders in the image reflects the range of writers – plus there are proportionately more females, as is the case for depression and ECT-treatment statistics. Looking out to the horizon is a symbol of hope. The sunset is a reflective image – it is welcome to see at the end of a day (or at the end of a journey) and metaphorically reflects the outcome of treatment.'* Milton even did some research on the choice of colours for the sky, using colours that represent hope. He considered the colour orange (in the shades between yellow and ochre/saffron) was most relevant to the message we wanted to give with the book, and the colour palette in this image was one of the combinations he found in a textbook on colours. Suddenly, all authors identified with the emotions evoked by the image.

Contents

	Introduction George Kirov	*page* 1
1.	A Mother's Journey Jan	7
2.	Rise Like a Phoenix Ruth	34
3.	'Young Men Don't Need ECT' CJ	50
4.	Back from the Edge Karen	63
5.	Two Sides of the Storm – A Couple's Story Sally and Paul	91
6.	The Long Way Home Lucy	103
7.	Surviving Bipolar – ECT and the 'Self-Binding Directive' Tania	112
8.	A Lifelong Struggle through Depression and Madness Liz	129
9.	Rollercoaster – My Ride from Suicide to Survival Berlinda	146

10.	The Doll's House Sue	157
11.	When Grief Breaks the Brain Jennifer	166
12.	The Making of *Waves of Hope* George Kirov	178

Introduction

'You still do that to people?'

This is a common question when I tell people what I do as an ECT consultant psychiatrist in our local hospital. Often, this is coupled with a look of bemusement, or even disapproval.

Electroconvulsive therapy (ECT) is the most controversial treatment in psychiatry and is an unknown area for most people. It has been nearly fifty years since *One Flew Over the Cuckoo's Nest* appeared on cinema screens, depicting Jack Nicolson undergoing a torturous treatment at the hands of the cruel Nurse Ratchet, yet this image persists in people's minds when ECT is mentioned. Depictions of a painful, barbaric, archaic treatment that can cause brain damage are at the forefront when ECT is suggested as an option for patients. This negative image persists, even among healthcare professionals: plenty of my colleagues are still perplexed by our role in the hospital. 'Does it even work?' they ask in wonder, as if we would continue to be employed if it did not.

ECT was first developed in Rome, in 1938, following observations that induced epileptic seizures could bring improvements in some mentally unwell patients. At that time, antidepressant and antipsychotic medications were not yet available, and it would be nearly two decades before these were developed. Patients with mental illnesses were largely living without any effective treatments, and when they became very unwell, they could stay unwell, with many of them confined in asylums.

ECT was found to be highly effective in patients suffering with schizophrenia or depression. The use of ECT rapidly spread around the world, as its effect was noted quickly by psychiatrists, who administered it to their patients. After the development of medications in the 1950s, the use of ECT began to decline, although it remains the most effective treatment for certain types of mental illness, such as psychotic depression and catatonia, as well as for many patients with mania, schizophrenia and depression who do not improve with other treatments. The use of ECT continued to decline over the years, after a strong backlash from groups that did not understand its role in modern psychiatry. The negative portrayal in the media also played a significant role.

Despite that, ECT has survived globally, to the present day, as it remains highly effective for those with very severe illness who do not improve with other treatments. In recent years, around 2,000 patients received ECT annually in the UK. The rate is higher in some European countries (for example, Sweden), but lower in others, such as Italy, the country where it was first developed. The majority of patients receiving ECT in the UK are treated for depressive episodes, with fewer for schizophrenia, mania and other conditions. Just over 40 per cent of depressed patients achieve remission (nearly complete absence of symptoms), while two-thirds of patients are rated as being 'much improved' or 'very much improved'. ECT is prescribed to twice as many women than men, reflecting the higher rate of depression among women. Elderly people are more likely to benefit from ECT, and the average age of those receiving ECT in the UK is just over sixty years.

This book was conceived with the view of lifting the mystery surrounding ECT and reducing the misinformation and hostility that abounds in the media and tarnishes public perception. We felt that the public should hear the voices of patients and their relatives, as it is not sufficient for doctors merely to describe the procedure and its benefits. This is why we brought together a group of people who were willing to share their stories, with each one writing a chapter. There is, admittedly, a higher proportion of good outcomes among the participants, compared to the statistics listed earlier, but not all outcomes are perfect and there are detailed descriptions of some of the side effects they experienced.

None of the contributors has been able to witness the procedure, since they were anaesthetised when ECT was given to them or, in the case of relatives, would have been asked to stay in the waiting room. This has resulted in a lack of technical descriptions of the procedure, so the following section provides a short summary of what happens during ECT in clinics in the UK. For a more detailed description, readers can access the patient information leaflet available on the Royal College of Psychiatrists website: www.rcpsych.ac.uk/mental-health/treatments-and-well being/ect.

What Is ECT?

The treatment is administered in hospital. The patient is given a short-acting general anaesthetic that is injected intravenously by a consultant anaesthetist. When the patient is fully asleep, they are given a short-acting muscle relaxant which reduces the strength of the muscle contractions. An electric current is passed through the head via two electrodes, typically one over each temple (bilateral ECT) or one over the right temple and one over the top of the head (right unilateral ECT). Right unilateral ECT causes less confusion and fewer memory problems. The muscle relaxant causes partial paralysis of the muscles, including those involved in breathing. As a result, the patient stops breathing and the anaesthetist delivers oxygen via a face mask. A foam mouthguard is inserted to prevent damage to the teeth. The electric stimulus consists of short pulses of electric current, each of 1/1,000 of a second or shorter, given for up to eight seconds. The amount of electricity required to induce an epileptic seizure varies between people, with older people requiring higher doses. The required dose changes during the course of treatment and is affected by certain medications that the patient may be taking. The electric current induces an epileptic seizure, which presents only with muscular twitches due to the partial paralysis caused by the muscle relaxant. Electroencephalogram (EEG) electrodes are attached to the head, to record the electrical activity in the brain. The modified seizure lasts typically between twenty seconds and one minute. Shorter seizures are less likely to be therapeutic, while those lasting more than two minutes should be stopped with medication.

In the UK the treatment is usually given twice a week, while in some countries, such as the USA, it is done three times a week. During the seizure, the blood pressure and pulse rate of the patient increase, and sometimes the pulse rate can become irregular. These changes are monitored and settle typically within a few minutes. The patient regains orientation after around fifteen to thirty minutes. Improvement in depression may start after only a few treatments. Recovery from depression is seen on average after eight sessions, but these numbers can vary quite widely between individuals. Relapses are common, with about half of all patients relapsing within twelve months. These patients might need additional courses of ECT, or a few additional sessions (continuation ECT), along with medications. A small proportion of patients who continue to relapse may require longer-term treatment (maintenance ECT), which can be given at intervals ranging between one and six weeks.

The most troubling side effect is temporary memory problems, reported by up to 40 per cent of patients while they are having ECT. Typically, people can forget some events that occurred during, or shortly before, the depression started and covering the time during the ECT course. For example, they may forget conversations with visitors during this time. Sometimes these memories return fully or partially, but in other cases these gaps can be permanent. A small proportion of people report some persistent memory loss for a number of months after the ECT. There are reports of patients who experienced gaps in memories stretching back for several years prior to the ECT course, and I have witnessed accounts of people who forgot some significant events that had happened several years before the treatment. The type and range of memory problems are covered extensively by the contributors throughout the book.

Despite its dramatic nature, the effects on the heart and the use of a general anaesthetic, the treatment is remarkably safe. Numerous brain imaging studies have shown that ECT doesn't cause brain damage and, if anything, there is evidence that it promotes new nerve growth in certain areas of the brain. This might play an instrumental role in how ECT works, although there are other potential mechanisms.

Patients who have capacity provide written consent before starting ECT. This is done after discussions with clinicians about the benefits and side effects of the treatment to support their informed consent. A large proportion of patients treated in the UK are so ill at the start of treatment that they are not able to make decisions about this treatment – that is, they lack capacity to consent. For such very ill patients (typically those who have become mute or are severely psychotic or disorientated), ECT can be given without consent, after a second opinion is given by an independent consultant psychiatrist. We hope that the information within this book will help some prospective ECT users make their informed decisions about this treatment.

These are the dry facts that you might hear from the psychiatrist. So, let us give the voice to the patients and their relatives, to see how things look from their point of view. I can promise that the tone will change, the emotions will become palpable, and you will learn a lot, just like I did.

George Kirov, October 2024

1

A Mother's Journey
Jan's Story

Part 1: 1999

4th May

I am thirty-one weeks pregnant with my first child. It is 5 o'clock in the morning and I awake to find my bed soaking wet. Knowing that urinary incontinence is not unusual in the later stages of pregnancy, at first I think I must have wet the bed. But there is a lot of liquid and it keeps coming. I begin to think that my waters may have broken. Up until this point, my pregnancy has been uneventful. Robert, my husband, and I have only just attended our first antenatal class and our baby is not due until July. I ask Robert what he thinks we should do; he reckons it is probably nothing as the baby is not due for another two months, and so I should just try to go back to sleep.

By 8 o'clock the liquid shows no signs of stopping, so I think it is best that I phone the maternity service at our local hospital.

'I'm thirty-one weeks pregnant and I think my waters may have broken', I say.

They tell me I need to go to the hospital. I do not quite understand the severity of the situation, so I ask if I should come sometime today.

The line is quiet for a second, a shocked pause in response to my lack of understanding.

'No. You need to come now.'

We pack ourselves into my silver Corsa Sport. I have nothing with me but a bag of sanitary pads as, what I now believe are my broken waters, are still flowing, and I presume I will be back home the same day.

We arrive at the hospital; my sanitary pad is getting increasingly sodden and heavy as we walk upstairs to the maternity ward. They take me for an ultrasound scan. After the scan the doctor comes in and says:

> 'You have a premature rupture of membranes. What this means is, most likely, you will go into labour imminently.'

1. A Mother's Journey

I am bewildered; my thoughts collide as I try to wrap my head around the situation. This is not my plan, I am supposed to be working until the start of July, I still have a conference that I am leading coming up, I have been working on it for months. Besides, we have taken only one antenatal class, the nursery is not ready, we have not bought most of what we need for the baby: no clothes, no nappies. None of this is supposed to be happening yet. I am not at all ready.

The doctor tells me that, as there are no signs of labour, I will be admitted to the antenatal ward. I will have scans on alternate days to see how long my pregnancy can be maintained. We are taken to see the special care baby unit. I am shocked by the sight of tiny, premature babies with their translucent skin, kept alive with tubes and wires.

The next two weeks are tempered, mainly, by a stirring mixture of anxiety and restless boredom. Each day is spent in anticipation of what the next monitoring or scan may show, with little else to do but sit on my bed in the mixed ante- and postnatal ward.

All day and night the shrill cries of newborns cut through the low, guttural shouts of women in early labour, backed by the rasp of struggling snores of exhausted new mothers. Despite the slowly rising humidity of mid-May, the heating is kept on high for the newborns not yet strong enough to maintain their body temperature. The room swelters in the thick hot air. Each night I lie awake, drenched in sweat as I struggle to peel the plastic sheets from my reddened skin.

18th May

It is 1 o'clock in the morning. A caesarean section has been planned for me later today. For the past twelve hours I have had dull nagging back pain. With the pain now intensifying, I press my bedside buzzer. A midwife comes to examine me and tells me that she thinks that I am going into labour. Following six hours of labour, I have an emergency caesarean section under general anaesthetic. Toby is born.

I have not yet seen my newborn son. I am confined to bed and hazy on morphine. Toby – four pounds, fourteen ounces and seven weeks premature – is in the special care baby unit. The midwives suggest that I should try to provide him with breast milk. I am given a small polaroid photo of my baby. Looking at this is intended to stimulate my breast milk. I am told that I will get the best supply of milk by using the breast pump every four hours throughout the day and night. The small quantity of creamy-yellow liquid that my body produces is given to Toby through a feeding tube.

Doctors tell us that Toby will remain in the special care baby unit until he meets three conditions: he must have regained his birth weight, be able to maintain his own body temperature and wake up at night to feed. This is likely to be close to his full-term date of 4th July.

23rd May

Five days after my caesarean section, I am sufficiently recovered to be able to go home. Still trying to maintain my breast milk, I set my clock radio alarm every three hours throughout the night. Sterilising the plastic bottle, breast pump funnel and tubing, then using the equipment, takes close to an hour. Each time, I go downstairs to my sitting room, assemble the pump paraphernalia on my coffee table and try to relax while listening to music. I always choose the same CD – Andrew Lloyd Webber's greatest hits. I listen to endless repetitions of 'Memories', 'Phantom of the Opera' and 'Don't Cry for me Argentina'.

1st June

My post-operative belly is tender, my caesarean scar is inflamed and oozing and my breasts are sore from the frequent pumping. Getting out of bed is increasingly wearisome and my body is struggling to produce sufficient milk.

1. A Mother's Journey

Toby, now fed with a combination of my breast milk and a formula designed for premature babies, is slowly gaining weight, having dropped to four pounds four ounces in the days following his birth. Despite not yet being back to his original weight or able to maintain his temperature, after two weeks in the special care baby unit, the hospital staff tell us he can go home. Toby should still have another five weeks in utero.

4th June

I have been awake for seventy-two hours. Before we left the hospital, three days earlier, the staff had explained that, unlike a full-term baby, Toby would not wake up to feed. It was made clear to us that, if we let our son sleep through the night without waking him, he would become very unwell. Gripped by fear that I will not be woken by my alarm clock, I do not sleep at all.

I do not feel tired because I am in a constant state of nervous anxiety. Robert is still on paternity leave, and it is a sunny June day, so I decide to go for a short walk alone. We live near a busy road, close to the motorway and, suddenly, I have an extraordinarily strong urge to run into the traffic. I have an overwhelming impulse to end my life. Shocked by the intensity of these unexpected feelings, I quickly return home. Robert arranges a visit from our GP, and we are told to go to a hospital, fifteen miles away, to see a psychiatrist.

I am very unkempt. My clothes are dirty: stained with food and breast milk and mismatched. I have not washed myself for days. My hair is tangled and greasy. The psychiatrist asks me how I am. I do not want to risk being admitted so I respond that I am very tired. I leave with a prescription for zopiclone – a tablet to help me sleep. Robert is looking after Toby in our bedroom and I am using our guest room so that I can rest undisturbed. The zopiclone works well. Some feelings of compulsion remain but I am certain that these will go once I have caught up on my sleep.

5th June

Robert has told my mum and dad that I am not well, and they make the three-hour drive from London to come and stay with us. When they arrive, mum asks me to make her a cup of tea. My mind races, I am shaking and I cannot concentrate. The task is impossible.

And then something very strange happens. It feels like there is an electrical thunderstorm inside my head. Buzzing with activity, zaps and flashes erupt within every part of my skull. The noise and energy of the thunder and lightning inside my brain is horrific, yet fascinating. I wonder if this is what it feels like to be put to death by electric chair. After fifteen minutes it stops, and I know that I have been irrevocably changed.

7th June

My hope for zopiclone-induced sleep has disappeared. After the first blissful night, the tablets have no effect and I am awake continuously. For three days and nights I talk to Robert non-stop. On the afternoon of the third day, Robert tells me that I will have to go back to the hospital. He says that, otherwise, I will make him so unwell that it is he who will need admitting.

8th June

I am admitted to a perinatal mental health bed. This is in a small two-bedded unit in the middle of a noisy acute psychiatric ward, but at least I can have Toby with me.

10th June

I spend my days drifting aimlessly, unable to concentrate on anything. I am deeply saddened by the knowledge that the electrical storm in my head a few days earlier has caused me to be brain-damaged. I realise that, with the damage to my brain being so severe, I cannot ever recover or live a normal life. I repeatedly explain to Robert and to mum and dad that something exceptional has happened to me – I am the only case in the world of someone having brain damage caused by an electrical storm in their head. Their unwillingness to acknowledge or accept the situation frustrates me immensely. My brain damage has caused me to be unable to concentrate or focus on anything other than this catastrophic injury and this is how I know it is real.

22nd June

Driven to despair by my belief that I will have to be in a hospital for ever because my condition is irreversible, I attempt to end my life.

23rd June

Following a night in the hospital's medical assessment ward, I am moved to the psychiatric intensive care unit (PICU). There are six beds in PICU – a mixture of male and female patients. On arrival, the nursing staff explain that, while they will try to keep me safe, I should know that PICU is a dangerous place and that there is every possibility that I will be assaulted.

PICU is not a suitable place for babies, so Toby is being cared for by my mum and dad at my home.

Due to the risk of escape attempts, there is no access to a place to sit outside the PICU, so I spend my time with the other patients in the smoking room. Everyone chain smokes and, consequently, we are always running out of cigarettes. One of the other patients, Vanessa, shows me that if you have Rizla papers you can use the discarded cigarette butts that people leave in the ashtray, open them up, get the tobacco out and make a roll up.

30th June

When I am not smoking, I spend my time writing. I am hopeful that, by reading my detailed account of the situation, the psychiatrist will recognise me as a new medical phenomenon. In preparation for the ward round, I spend hours crafting my letter to her. I am excited for my meeting and, when the time comes, I present my copious sheets of paper. To my utmost frustration and dismay, she does not read any of it.

7th July

Our midday lunch is nearly over. As usual, the plastic knives, forks and spoons are collected in by staff and carefully counted in case any of the patients attempt to hide them to use for self-harm. A nurse asks to see me and tells me the doctor has decided that I am well enough to return to the main ward. I am surprised because I feel no different to the day of my admission to PICU. My despair about having irreversible catastrophic brain damage, and my consequent drive to die as the only way out, is as strong as ever.

8th July

I go for my usual breakfast of toast and marmalade in the ward dining room. As I sit down, Vanessa approaches me. She had left the PICU two days before me. Without warning, she smacks me hard across the face and I am knocked to the ground.

9th July

Back on the ward, Toby is with me again: resulting in more tasks that I struggle to undertake. The staff insist that I must make up Toby's formula bottles myself. I find this very difficult because my hands shake constantly; the formula powder mainly goes on the floor and my hands are frequently scalded by boiling water that I attempt to pour from the kettle.

I have decided to ask for ECT. I know nothing about ECT other than what I have seen on television dramas. Having been in hospital for a month now, and still feeling as bad as I did in early June, I think it might be worth a go. I request to see the psychiatrist that day, and, unusually, my request is granted.

I choose my words badly.

'I want to have my brain fried', I say.

'What do you mean?' she asks.

'I want that treatment where your brain is electrocuted', I respond.

She asks me why I want ECT, and I explain that, as nothing else has worked, I think it would be worth trying. She tells me this is a terrible idea and that there is no way she will agree to it.

12th July

Time on the ward passes excruciatingly slowly. Unable to read or watch television, I spend my days sitting in the small lounge adjacent to my mother-and-baby bed. In the mornings, this is with one of the two nursery nurses provided by the hospital. At midday either my mum and dad or Robert's mum arrive to spend time with Toby and me. Every evening, Robert comes to the hospital on his way home from work. I try to look pleased to see my visitors on their daily trips. Actually, I feel nothing except constant despair.

The antipsychotic and antidepressant medications that I have taken since the day of my admission make no difference to me. But one thing does help somewhat – the little blue pill – lorazepam. Lorazepam does not remove my feelings of despair, but it does, for a couple of hours, take the edge off.

The doctors have prescribed me lorazepam as 'PRN', meaning that it should be provided to the patient as required. Lorazepam is highly addictive and nursing policy seems to be to refuse my requests for it on that basis. Given that I do not intend to stay alive in the long term, certainly no longer than the time it will take me to work out my next suicide attempt, the possibility of long-term addiction is not a concern to me.

It is very frustrating to have my requests for the one thing that brings me relief almost constantly turned down, but it is only when I get talking to a couple of other patients, that I understand how to change this. They explain that the way to get lorazepam is to kick off. The staff do not want patients shouting, swearing and being aggressive. Despite my immense anguish, I have been keeping this to myself. The next time one of the nurses asks me how I am, I start shouting and swearing. I am rewarded with the little blue pill. Now that I know the route to temporary relief, I intend to use it whenever I feel overwhelmed.

17th July

The mid-summer weather is good and I am permitted to go for walks in the hospital grounds accompanied by staff or my family members. I am also allowed occasional home leave. Being outside or at home does not change what is going on in my head, or my level of despair, but it is better than being stuck on the ward.

Today, being Saturday, I have been given six hours of home leave, so Robert collects Toby and me from the ward and we go back to our home. I spend a lot of time pacing. Then, in the kitchen cupboard, I spot a full bottle of Talisker whisky. This is Robert's favourite. Desperate for even momentary relief I decide that a stiff drink might help. I pour myself a large measure and gulp it. Having not drunk alcohol for many months, I expect the effects to come quickly. I want to feel my anxiety drifting away. The first glass does nothing. So, I pour another, an even larger measure this time. Soon, I am halfway down the bottle and I still feel no different. By the end of the afternoon, and the time to return to the hospital, only about one-fifth of the bottle of Talisker remains undrunk. Under normal circumstances, this amount of alcohol would make me very drunk, very sleepy and very nauseated. Yet I am completely untouched. More proof that my brain no longer functions in the way it used to.

24th July

Saturday again. Robert picks up Toby and me in the morning and we set off home. It is a cloudless, sunny day and, together with mum and dad, we decide to go out for a walk and a picnic. Toby does not seem quite right. Usually, he has a good appetite but today he is not interested in his bottle. He is not very alert and he is making some strange moaning noises. Everyone agrees he is just a little out of sorts. The day passes. I am in my bedroom at home getting ready to return to the hospital. Suddenly, although he is no different from earlier, I feel that I need to take Toby to a doctor urgently. This will make our return to the hospital ward late and will overstay the amount of leave that the psychiatrist has permitted me for the day. I am so insistent though that Robert agrees, and we take Toby to the general practice out of hours service. We see Dr Singh. He is a GP that I work with and, initially, he greets me with a warm smile. Then he sees Toby.

'You must get him to the hospital immediately', he says.

'There's no time to wait for an ambulance. You must drive there. I'll phone ahead and let them know you're on your way.'

On arrival, we are rushed through to a resuscitation room in the paediatric intensive care unit and Toby is surrounded by medical staff. One of the doctors tells us that Toby is extremely poorly and at this point they do not know what the outcome will be. I am now extremely late for my required return to the ward.

Then we are told that, because Toby is so poorly, Robert and I will stay in the parent rooms next to the paediatric intensive care unit and that this has been agreed by my psychiatrist. A nurse explains that they think that Toby has meningitis. He is attached to multiple pieces of equipment, but the main course of treatment is intravenous antibiotics. The next twenty-four hours will be critical and they tell us to prepare for the worst. I feel no emotion. It is as if I am looking in on somebody else's life. I understand that what is happening is serious and could have a tragic outcome, yet I do not feel it.

25th July

Robert's mum and dad have travelled down to the hospital so now there are six of us around Toby's cot side. We are told that Toby will need a lumbar puncture and I ask to stay with him while this is carried out. My request is refused.

26th July

Doctors tell us that Toby does not have meningitis. He has a double bacterial pneumonia, will remain in hospital for a few more days and a full recovery is expected.

27th July

As the days pass, I am aware that, once Toby is out of danger, I will be returned to the psychiatric hospital. I prefer the paediatric ward because I have more freedom and the food is better.

30th July

The day that Toby is to be discharged has arrived. I am acutely aware that every hour brings my return to the ward closer. Then, to my astonishment, I am told that because I have been doing so well while Toby has been on the intensive care unit, it has been decided that I no longer need to be a psychiatric inpatient and am therefore discharged.

6th August

I had hoped that, by being released from detention under the Mental Health Act, I would start to feel a little better: as if having my physical freedom would untether me from my mental torment. Yet, this past week has been little different from a week on the ward. Anxious that it is unsafe to leave me on my own, Robert has arranged for his mum or my mum and dad to stay with me at our house all the time. I am still unable to focus on anything, so I wander about the house and in and out of the garden. Mostly, I start my day by running a bath, pouring in some of my favourite bubbles. But, by the time I get in, I have lost interest and pull the plug almost immediately. Each day passes very slowly: an endless loop of mealtime and sleeping time.

1. A Mother's Journey

11th August

Today there is a total eclipse of the sun, visible from my home. This is the only day it will occur in Britain during my lifetime. I am unmoved.

15th September

More than six weeks after my discharge from hospital, little has changed. I remain under the constant watchful eye of people who love me and are determined to keep me from harm. I feel deeply resentful that every attempt I make to go out alone, or evade their company, is thwarted.

Today I am due to go to the outpatient clinic and meet my new psychiatrist. This is the first time I have seen a doctor since leaving hospital in July. I know how I will play this meeting – say little and give nothing away. Above all, do not say or do anything that might give them cause to suggest a readmission.

There are two male doctors in the consulting room. One is middle-aged, with sandy hair and a beard. The other dark haired and younger. Neither is the consultant: they explain that the consultant is currently away on holiday but is one of the most eminent psychiatrists in the country and an expert in perinatal psychiatry. This consultant has set up a mother-and-baby day unit, they explain, which is recognised as one of the best facilities in the UK.

Despite my intentions, I find myself drawn into speaking. Encouraged by their rapt attention and precipitous nodding, I explain how I had believed that I was brain-damaged and that this was what had led me to attempt suicide. I strenuously deny that I still believe this and adamantly refute any suggestion that I am still thinking of ending my life – I am acutely aware that what I say risks a response that I am very keen to avoid.

I am astonished when sandy doctor tells me that, given my belief that I was brain-damaged, it is entirely reasonable that this would have made me want to end my life. He is the first person who does not tell me my thinking was clearly nonsense: he simply agrees that a logical thought, for someone who believed they were catastrophically brain-damaged, would be to want to die.

He asks me what I would find helpful.

I explain about the little blue pills and how since these are the only medication that I have found of any benefit, how frustrating it has been to have these denied to me. I am expecting the usual narrative of how addictive these are and that I cannot have any. But sandy doctor is one step ahead of me. He tells me that, if Robert takes charge of the tablets, I can have a supply of lorazepam: one tablet up to four times a day.

Then he asks me what I want to happen next.

This is something I have been pondering for a while. The last time I felt fully normal was while I was at work, in April 1999, before the night that my waters had broken prematurely and the stress and sleepless nights that followed.

I can now see only two possible ways forward. Either I attempt to recreate routine and focus by returning to work, or I find a way to end my life. Of course, I am not going to tell sandy doctor of my latter thought, so I tell him that my maternity leave is due to finish at the end of September and that I want to go back to work.

Sandy doctor seems surprised and suggests that this would be a high-risk approach, as I may not be able to cope at work. However, as a compromise, he agrees that I can go back to work half time from the start of October, as long as I attend the mother-and-baby day unit every afternoon.

31st October

Halloween. I have chosen a large and well-shaped pumpkin and have set about carefully carving it into a lantern. I put a couple of tea lights in, pick Toby up and show him the glimmering flames. Toby is five and a half months old now, interested in everything: a very smiley, lively and cuddly little boy.

I have been back at work for a month. Some days I have struggled with my concentration and my anxiety has started to rise. At those times, I have found that taking a little blue pill has helped and has enabled me to remain at my desk.

As agreed with sandy doctor, I have been going into the office in the mornings, picking up Toby from nursery at lunchtime, then spending the afternoons at the mother-and-baby day unit. The staff there are kind, understanding, not judgemental. I have made friends with some of the other patients. Sometimes we do activities: crafts or baking; sometimes there are talks about parenting skills or first aid; other times we just relax and chat. The room is welcoming, with comfortable sofas, play mats for the babies and a never-ending supply of hot drinks and biscuits. I feel safe here.

It will still take some time for me to fully recover. Now though, I am confident that I will be well again, that I will be able to reduce, and then come off, all my medication over time and that Robert, Toby and I will, at last, be a family.

Part Two: 2016

27th July

I am enjoying my summer holiday in Venice with Toby, now aged seventeen, Alicia and Lily – my twin girls, who were born in November 2002. On finding out I was pregnant again in April 2002, I had been referred to a specialist perinatal mental health service. I was fortunate that my GP practice had an attached clinical psychologist. With her, I looked at my potential risk factors for severe mental illness and developed an advance directive. A friend, Paula, who was a hospital social worker, agreed to be my advocate should I need one. A visit was set up for me to look around a local mother-and-baby perinatal mental health unit. My GP made arrangements that, if I should become unwell out of hours, those services would also know the plan. I had been well prepared.

Following my daughters' birth, a planned caesarean section that went smoothly, I remained well, so I was relieved and happy to think that my illness after the birth of my son was a one-off event in my life.

Cycling around Venice Lido with my three children, I feel good. Strong and healthy. The years since my postnatal illness with Toby had been eventful: I had undergone major emergency surgery; one of my closest friends had passed away following a stage four cancer diagnosis; my mother-in-law had died unexpectedly; and Robert and I had divorced when our daughters were nine. I had managed the stresses of these events, with the help of my friends, and I had not had any psychiatric admissions or contact with mental health services.

In April of this year, I experienced a few weeks of hypomania. Seeking an appointment with one of the GPs at the local practice, I had entered his consulting room, told him I felt 'wired' and had declined the offer of a seat before pacing his room. I had asked lots of questions about the pictures on the walls, suggesting that these were actually of the devil. I left with a prescription for a low dose of an antipsychotic medication and, after two months of taking this, I felt back to normal.

The Venice holiday – sightseeing and relaxing with Toby, Alicia and Lily – feels just what I need to recharge prior to returning to my work as head of department and my busy life as a single parent.

4th August

My first day back at work following two weeks off. Driving to my workplace, I feel a little nervous. I am anxious about what might have happened at work while I was on holiday: the hundreds of emails that await me, catching up with the backlog and picking up my on-call duty requiring me to be available twenty-four hours a day for the whole of the next week.

Exchanging the usual pleasantries with my colleagues, I walk across the open plan office to my desk. As I switch on my laptop, and emails flood into the inbox, suddenly I feel overwhelmed and terrified. This is not something I have experienced before. My mind starts racing.

Two of my team members ask to talk to me about a serious service issue. I listen intently to what they are saying but it is unintelligible to me. They are asking for my advice about something, and I have nothing to suggest. I have no coherent thoughts.

24th August

Three weeks have passed in a blur. I am barely managing two hours per night of sleep, I cannot eat and I have no concentration. Work tasks that I would have completed with ease before my holiday feel confusing and insurmountable. I cannot do any of the household chores that I need to carry out. In desperation, I try anything that might help. I have relinquished my morning cafetiere and started drinking camomile tea. I have attempted some gardening, some yoga postures, a run in the countryside. The calm from each lasts for only a few minutes before my thoughts overwhelm me. I tell my mum that I feel as bad as I did in 1999.

In the office, unable to focus on my own work, I invite myself to meetings that my team members are leading. I do not have anything to contribute, and it must appear very strange to them, but I cannot bear sitting at my desk, staring at my computer screen full of documents and emails that I have no ability to read.

I arrange an urgent appointment with my GP. I intend to request a short-term prescription of Valium to reduce my anxiety. The doctor is reluctant to agree to my request but, after a long talk, I leave with a prescription, a referral to the community mental health team and advice to take the rest of the week off.

30th August

The Valium has not had the effect I had hoped. Anxiety has become a constant feature of my waking hours. The little sleep I do get is in brief spells interspersed with vivid nightmares. I spend my days huddled in a blanket on my cream leather recliner armchair. I use alcohol to seek relief from the whirling thoughts.

Convinced that I am suffering from work related anxiety, and that, if I can get that under control, I will be back at work in the next week or two, I see the GP again. He asks me how much alcohol I am drinking. I lie and tell him it is about half a bottle of wine a day. I say I am improving and that I want to go back to work but he refuses to sign me as fit and refers me to the crisis team.

31st August

Alicia and Lily persuade me to take them to the ice cream parlour: a five-minute walk away. I do not want to leave the house. The effort of putting on my shoes and picking up my handbag feels too hard. But they are insistent, and I do not have the energy to explain why I will not go with them.

I need money so I go to the cash machine on the way and request £200 – the maximum I can withdraw. Arriving at the ice cream shop, I discover I have left the money at the bank and, when I return, it has gone.

1st September

I agree to daily visits from the intensive home-based treatment team (IHTT). I decide to make a phone call to the employee assistance programme helpline: a support and advice service offered to all staff where I work. I begin to explain that I am stressed about work, that I am hoping to find some techniques that will help, with a view to returning to work next week. The telephone counsellor asks whether

I am currently receiving any other support and I explain about the crisis team and the IHTT. Initial silence at the other end of the line, then the counsellor tells me that I am not suitable for the service and the call comes to an abrupt end.

At the start of my time off work, I was buying food and preparing simple meals for my children. This has now become impossible due to my level of agitation. Toby is due to start his second year of sixth-form college this week. Alicia and Lily are returning to their third year at high school. One of them must have phoned their dad to tell him what has been happening because Robert arrives at my door and insists that he is taking the kids, and me, to his house.

6th September

It feels very strange staying in Robert's house: we have not slept under the same roof since our separation in 2011. Paula – my close friend and work colleague, who supported me during my pregnancy with Alicia and Lily – comes round to take my laptop and work phone away. I am angry about this unnecessary intrusion given that I am hoping to return to work next week. I tell Paula that I need to go to the shops to buy a hairbrush, so we walk into town. I already have a hairbrush at Robert's house but going to the supermarket gives me an opportunity to buy wine. It is 10 o'clock in the morning.

My fixation on returning to work is driven by my situation: as a single parent with a mortgage and bills to pay, my income is essential. My employee sickness benefits are generous – full pay for the first six months of absence – and my mum and dad have the means to help me financially if I need them to. Yet, I have become convinced that if I do not return to work imminently, I will be sacked; my lack of income will lead to the loss of my house, and then to homelessness and destitution.

12th September

Another GP appointment, the usual format. The doctor asks me how I am. I reply that I am fine, just a little stressed about work and that I think this will improve when I go back. He tells me I am quite unwell and will probably not be able to return for a number of weeks. He asks whether he can check my weight and notes that I have lost half a stone in the past fortnight. He asks about my drinking. My standard response: 'a couple of glasses of wine'. His face tells me he does not believe me and he says I really need to stop drinking or, at the very least, cut right back. We agree to meet again in a week's time.

17th September

I have been phoning the IHTT every day this week. Each morning I wake up feeling terrified and count the minutes until their phone line opens and I can call them to explain how I feel. I am aware that I am very repetitive on these daily phone calls and the team seem to be losing patience with me.

By Saturday, I have decided it is time for me to leave Robert's house and go back to my own home. Using the opportunity of everyone being out except Lily, I run out of the front door and into the road. Lily runs after me and persuades me to go back inside. I go to my bedroom and then, around midday, I get called to the sitting room where I am introduced to two doctors and a social worker. They ask me lots of questions. I know I must have answered in a reasonable way because they leave. This is a relief. I had been concerned they might want to talk to me about a hospital admission.

Later that afternoon, my friends Heidi and Lara come round. I do not remember them saying they planned to visit but my memory has not been good, and I am happy to see them. We settle on the sofa, and they start chatting. The doorbell goes. The two doctors and the social worker from the morning walk into the lounge and sit down. This is an unwelcome turn of events, and I will have to do some quick thinking to get them to go away again. They ask me how I am and whether I have any thoughts of self-harm. I repeat my well-rehearsed story. I am fine, just a little anxious about work. The sitting room is full of people now – Robert, Toby, Alicia, Lily, Heidi and Lara. The social worker asks them whether they agree with what I am saying. To my annoyance and dismay, they all say that they think I am very unwell and getting worse. One of the doctors asks me whether I am willing to accept a voluntary admission to hospital. Realising my options are limited, I ask what will happen if I decline. The only choice on offer is between a voluntary admission and a compulsory one. Reluctantly, I agree to go voluntarily.

I am presented with another choice. Mental health beds are in short supply. I am asked whether I would prefer to go to a working-age adult ward fifty miles away or an elderly mental health ward ten miles away. I am forty-eight. I do not want to be on a ward where the next closest person to my age will be in their late sixties. But my top priority is being somewhere that my children and my friends can visit me, so I agree to go with the old people.

The decision is made. The doctors leave quickly, while the social worker remains and says he will drive me to the hospital in his car. A discussion ensues about who will go with me. I want Toby to come. We are walking down the drive when Toby gets called back and told that, as he is seventeen, he is not old enough to go. Heidi and Lara come with me instead and sit either side of me in the back of the car. It is midnight when we arrive at the hospital for, what I intend to be, a very short stay.

28th September

Robert and five of my closest friends have formed a WhatsApp support group. Between them they form a rota so that I have visitors nearly every day. Today is Jessica's turn to visit me. Jessica runs a successful business and I explain to her that I am not mentally unwell, just stressed by my inability to do my usual job. I tell her I am a good worker and suggest that she employs me. To my chagrin she does not take me up on my offer. Perhaps as a consolation, she asks me if I would like to go out for the day on Sunday. I suggest we visit Scarborough.

2nd October

Today is very cold and windy but I am looking forward to my trip to the seaside with Jessica. I think the grey autumn North Sea may provide an opportunity to bring an end to things.

While I am waiting for Jessica to arrive, I head off to the local supermarket, which is just around the corner from the hospital. Whenever I am allowed time off the ward on my own, I go there to buy alcohol. My black leather handbag is large enough to carry three little bottles of wine. My bag is never searched so I can bring whatever I want onto the ward. Arriving back in my room, I drink directly from the bottle, quickly, to get through all three before Jessica arrives.

Our visit to Scarborough passes uneventfully. Despite the perishing wind, the seaside town is packed with people, rendering an escape attempt impossible.

4th October

Early evening. It has been decided, without notice, that I will move to the working-age adults' ward. I am told my behaviour has been upsetting some of the older people and my removal has been prompted by an incident where I had thrown the hard black plastic chairs around the dining room.

The ward staff enter my bedroom and start shoving my possessions into plastic bags. It is inevitable that my carefully hidden stash of things that might be useful in a suicide attempt are found. The staff do not challenge me on my contraband. However, shortly after my move to the working-age adults ward, I am informed that I am now detained under the Mental Health Act.

18th October

I have been given a diagnosis of psychotic depression and have been treated with high doses of antipsychotic and antidepressant medication for over a month. I do not believe this diagnosis and the lack of effect of the medication confirms my belief. There is no change in my state of mind, and my despair and suicidal ideation remain continuous. Robert asks the psychiatrist whether there could be any link between my illness after Toby was born and this episode seventeen years later, given that I am now in perimenopause, with the hormonal turbulence this brings. He is told that there is no link between the two.

I am pleased that Robert has been told that my current admission and my postnatal illness are not related. My belief is that I am not mentally ill. I have work related stress that has got a little out of hand. I try, repeatedly, to impress this on everybody who comes to visit me. I am not unwell. I should not be held under section. I should not be on a psychiatric ward.

26th October

On the ward I join in the therapy activities: crafts, a weekly trip to the bowling alley, walks. I am given a mindfulness tape to listen to. With continuous, mind-racing thoughts about how I will be imminently homeless, the mindfulness tape is not helpful. I rarely talk to the ward staff. The staff spend most of their time in the ward office so any opportunity to talk is extremely limited. There is nothing I wish to tell them. I do not think sharing my thoughts will help to secure my discharge.

I use the weekly ward round as an opportunity to explain that I feel much better and that I want more time away from the hospital. I am surprised, but delighted, when my request for overnight home leave is granted.

A friend agrees to stay with me at my home for the night.

27th October

At 10 o'clock the next morning I am picked up by the police, wandering shoeless on the hard shoulder of the M1. I had been on my way to visit mum and dad when I had collided into the central reservation. The airbags had gone off, bruising my shoulder and cutting my face, but I had continued driving until my car ran out of fuel.

After being checked over in Accident and Emergency, I am taken to a room at the hospital – a place of safety – and told I am being held under Mental Health Act section 136. Two police officers guard me. I am very cold as I am wearing cropped jeans and a t-shirt, and it is late October. Fortunately, my friend Heidi has been visiting family close by and is able to bring me some warm things to wear.

In the early evening, I am transported by ambulance back to the mental health ward.

Late October to Mid-February 2017

My memories of this period are sparse. There are days and weeks of which I remember nothing. I have some snapshot scenes in my head from this time, like a glimpse of a photograph, but no more.

I do know from those few glimpses, from my friends and family, and from reading my GP notes, that I made two suicide attempts. The first, in November, resulted in an admission to an acute medical ward for twenty-four hours. The second, in December, lead to an admission for a week. I was convinced that I was going to be forever stuck in the same unbearable, tormented state. It was this belief that made me feel I could not carry on.

My friends have told me of my 'manic phoning phase'. For a few weeks, I spent most of each day repeatedly phoning every contact on my iPhone.

One of the few memories I do have of these months is being offered ECT. I cannot say exactly when this was, but I do remember signing the consent form. I did not believe that ECT would help. Multiple courses of different combinations of medication had been tried, all with no effect. I had no reason to think ECT would make any difference to me. But I had nothing to lose so I would have accepted anything that was offered to me.

The effect of ECT was remarkable. After only a couple of sessions, friends who visited were astounded by the changes in me. One of my closest friends was sceptical at first, but later described seeing a difference in me almost after the first session. She said I started to look more alive, the colour came back into my cheeks, and I seemed much more able to follow conversation. I was not fully back to my old self but, they tell me, I was, in some respects, me again.

Mid-February

I am coming to the end of my course of twelve ECT sessions. For each session, I am taken to a hospital a few miles away which has an ECT suite. Before each trip, a doctor examines me to make sure I am physically well enough to have the treatment. The ward has an agency nurse. A big Scottish guy – Andy. He has been designated to go with me for my ECT. He seems kind and we chat. At the ECT suite I am given a general anaesthetic and then come round with a coffee in the recovery room before Andy and I are transported back to the ward. I sleep most of the afternoon.

As I improve, I become more aware of my surroundings and more able to talk to other patients. Staff members spend much of their shift in the ward office. There appears to be little general observation of, or interaction with, patients. The ward is a tinder box. I see emotions escalating in other people, resulting in an ever-heightening atmosphere. Often things reach boiling point, and the result is the inevitable screaming, shouting, swearing, sometimes violence. When the staff alarms sound, everything gets very hectic and noisy until those kicking off are either bundled into the seclusion room or forcibly sedated. As a patient, all I can do is either retreat to my room or just sit tight until things become calm again.

6th March

The day of my discharge from the hospital. For the past two weeks I have been allowed home for a succession of overnight stays and now, nearly six months after it began, the end of my hospital stay has come.

20th March

My first day back at work. I have been away on sickness absence for 200 days.

Getting back to work is important. I need the structure and routine that being at work gives me, and I want the opportunity to bring some normality back to my life. My return has been carefully planned. I have had a long appointment with the occupational health physician, who has worked out a return-to-work plan with me and a phased return.

20th June

Going back to work has been difficult. My confidence in myself is extremely low. The medication I need to take is slowing my thought processes and my concentration is reduced.

In meetings I am slow to react meaning that, often, by the time I have thought about what I want to say, the discussion has moved on. Writing my first report takes ages and I just cannot get it right. On a couple of days, I have felt so stressed by lunchtime that I end up taking the afternoon off.

November

Toby is in his first year at university, 100 miles away. Alicia and Lily are finally living with me again most of the time. I am still finding work hard. My concentration is reduced and my ability to make decisions is impaired. I have spoken to my union to ask whether I might be eligible for ill-health retirement, but they tell me this is very unlikely.

July 2018

Nice, South of France. I am on holiday with Toby, Alicia and Lily. In December I had requested a move to a lower-banded post at work to reduce my stress levels. I am now very much enjoying my new role, as deputy head of department. I have rebuilt my social life, spending time with friends and family.

It is a balmy summer's day, and we are on the rooftop bar of our hotel. I look out to the sea and feel happy.

2

Rise Like a Phoenix
Ruth's Story

2. Rise Like a Phoenix

I adore live musical theatre. When I heard that Conchita, the bearded drag diva (!) who won the 2014 Eurovision Song Contest, was going to perform a concert at the London Palladium a few years later, I had to invite my sister to come to it with me. Hearing, that evening, the powerful, winning ballad 'Rise Like a Phoenix' gave us the opportunity to celebrate, together, the transformation I had been so fortunate to experience in 2014: the end of a very dark time and of regaining my life.

Today, I am a busy and contented woman with a very kind and loving husband, an extremely caring, close family, a portfolio of highly interesting work, and I enjoy sharing some of the wisdom that my middle-age experience brings. I've travelled to many countries in my life and I'm aware that life, itself, certainly is a journey. Mine has mostly been great; however, sadly, along the way I have had two episodes of severe depressive disorder and, each time, extreme agitation and frightening psychosis have featured.

As a young child, it's fair to say that I was precocious, a worrier and perfectionist – always wanting to do the right thing. Born the eldest of four children in the late 1960s to free-thinking and adventurous young parents, I took upon myself a mantle of care. When I was nearly four, my parents, toddler brother and I lived in a small town in the countryside in Argentina for a year. Life there was quite dramatic and, although I was very young, I have a good memory for details. Very soon after we arrived, my mother was seriously ill for a number of weeks and was ordered to take bed rest. With my father at work, my brother and I were cared for by a very kind Polish immigrant neighbour, although I still spent quite a lot of time playing quietly at home in the garden or in my mother's room, content in my own company. I loved then – and still love – nature and spent happy hours alone closely studying beautiful, colourful flowers, birds and insects in the garden around our house. In the house, there is a particularly striking moment that stands out in my memory; I was sitting and staring long and hard at myself in my parents' wardrobe mirror and was overcome with an unsettling sensation of really wondering to myself 'Who am I?' – an early existential experience.

My anxious nature was often evident during this time. On several occasions after we had settled, my parents decided to take us to see more of the country. One was a six-week, family road trip by car: wild camping in the remote Andes. One day, when we were far from any inhabited places, I anxiously asked my parents what would happen if we broke down or ran out of fuel. The reply of 'Yes, I wonder?' from one of them wasn't at all the practical or helpful answer I expected to allay my fear. At other times we had to make dangerous river crossings and I can still recall, now, looking out at the fast-moving water swirling around the car, terrified it was going to start to seep in under our feet as we headed towards the deepest centre point and that we would be washed away down the water's course. Some experiences, closer to home, also put fear in me at this time: the old woman at an outdoor party, late one night, who aggressively warned us children not to poke a beetle we were watching or it would blind us; the week-long build up to carnival night when we would go to watch 'the man who has buried himself alive' reappear; and, most chilling of all, being lifted up to peep inside the macabre, ornate, dusty, old, gothic, black funeral carriage kept in a corner of the village cemetery when we went to see families laying flowers there on Day of the Dead. We had to leave an Argentina suddenly and, for us children, with no warning, just over a year after we arrived, due to political unrest. We were hidden under blankets in the middle of the night and driven away. I grieved all I had loved about life there for a long time and was always determined to go back one day.

Back in England, when I was pre-teen, I had times when I felt genuine waves of depression. Historical drama series on television, typically on Sunday evenings, with stories of frequent, terrifying

2. Rise Like a Phoenix

illness and other morbid dangers, haunted me. Watching the news and other serious documentary programmes would trigger my worries and I often thought, but didn't talk, about huge issues – cancer, nuclear holocaust and death – whilst I'm fairly sure most of my friends were happily dressing their dolls, swapping stickers and solving the Rubik's cube.

My mother, her mother and, perhaps, previous generations in our family experienced crippling periods of depression, at intervals, during their lives. My mother's own awareness of her illness meant that she was able to support me on the occasions when I shared how I felt, but I often struggled on silently when spells of depression crept up on me. For example, as an undergraduate student at Oxford University I was very insecure and experienced imposter syndrome about my academic ability throughout my studies. It was the mid-1980s, the start of the AIDS epidemic, and I also became hyper-vigilant about hygiene. For some years, I struggled with an obsessive compulsion to wash my hands, afraid I was a source of contamination. It developed into quite a ritual; washing my hands in a particular way would confirm, in my mind, that I wouldn't be harmful to anyone I came in contact with. I developed a few other rituals when particularly stressed during my twenties: checking and rechecking I'd locked doors, shut windows and turned off switches and gas. Sometimes I was compelled to return after leaving in order to go through all the checks again and calm my anxiety. Some years later, I developed a fear of lit candles and once drove from my own house to my parents' late at night to look through the window and check that they didn't have any candles burning. It wasn't until many years later, whilst watching a documentary about obsessive compulsive disorder (OCD) with my father, that I broke down in tears and shared, for the first time with anyone, my own experience.

As an undergraduate, I also had my first serious relationship with a fellow student, a charming but highly manipulative fantasist; a bad break up followed – just before the pressure of my final exams.

Another depressive wave came over me when I was working in my first job, living away from home and very much an outsider in a close-knit, ex-mining community. Ten years later, working hard in a job with quite a high level of stress and significant managerial responsibility, living alone in my own home, I sank again as I tried to process, by myself, the shocking events of the twin towers attack and not feeling that I could talk to anyone about this.

None of these episodes of depression lasted more than a matter of weeks, thankfully, and I can't remember if I needed medication to help recover. However, in late 2003, I chose to take a career break before deciding which direction to take next. This was going to be the exciting gap year of world travel that I hadn't previously been able to afford years before when university friends had invited me to join them travelling after we graduated. I was in my mid-thirties when I embarked on a solo six-month trip around the world.

I made detailed plans, before setting out, to visit family and friends on my travels: cousins in Australia, a university friend in Tasmania and three months travelling around New Zealand with stays in the homes of family friends and their relations. In between these homestays, I joined tours and stayed in hostels, meeting many other travellers. I often felt bereft when, after meeting lovely, like-minded people for a short time, we would have to say farewell abruptly. It was also very physically and mentally tiring to have to take care of myself and possessions; continually moving, making arrangements and managing my savings effectively so I would budget correctly for the entire trip. By the time I reached Auckland, after four months of travelling, this was starting to really affect me mentally, but I had always had a dream to experience a tropical island, and booked and flew to the Cook Islands for a stay of two weeks. Unfortunately, I wasn't prepared for the cultural and practical differences of remote, isolated island life even if it is considered a pacific paradise. I had arranged to stay in a simple backpackers' bungalow in a hostel complex near the one main road which circled the coast of Rarotonga, the main island. This was a lively place, but I struggled to socialise with other, mainly young, travellers as I normally would. It's clear to me now that depression was already getting a grip and making me unusually reclusive.

As a trained teacher, I had hoped to offer to do some voluntary work in a primary school on the island, but I only managed a couple of sessions as I was becoming very anxious and agitated. This was greatly exacerbated by an incident on the second day of my stay. I took the hourly island bus to one of the stunning, white sand beaches for a swim. I arrived early before the sun was intense but, after my swim, a solo backpacking holidaymaker asked me if I would watch his bag and clothes whilst he went snorkelling. He was gone a long time, my bus arrived but I missed it whilst I dutifully stayed and kept guard, feeling again my sense of responsibility as I had continued to do so since a I was a very young child. Although I was in the shade of the fringe of palm trees, I didn't realise that I was getting sunburnt from the reflected rays until later back at the bungalow. With my legs red and hot, I felt overwhelming waves of panic and fear. Wide publicity, at the time, of the dangerous hole in the ozone layer, the Aussie mantra to 'Slip, Slap, Slop' and warnings to stay out of the sun during the middle of the day played in a loop in my head. My shins felt on fire, and I berated myself constantly for my stupidity, fearing that I had put myself in danger of UV damage and skin cancer. I made a telephone box call back to my family at home who assured me it was probably not at all as bad as I thought, since I hadn't developed any blistering. Despite this, I couldn't keep a more rational perspective on the situation and was sure I needed to visit a doctor. At night my anxiety and the heat stopped me from sleeping. I got up several times to take showers, lay on my bed obsessing and continued to lose a grip on reality through lack of sleep.

Although it was a big drain on my funds, after a couple of days I moved to an air-conditioned luxury beach resort with friendly owners, P and D. D took me to see the pleasant, relaxed local doctor who listened, nodding and smiling slightly whilst I gave my (now frantic) explanation of the problem. He gave me standard practical advice for calming the immediate sunburn and taking care in the future, but my mind was still in turmoil about the serious damage I was convinced I had done to my skin. I shut myself away in the idyllic, beachside chalet, berating myself for my stupidity and hardly venturing out so that P, D and the other guests must have wondered about my continuing, very odd behaviour.

Although I was in a high state of agitation and irrational fear, I made it back to New Zealand to complete several more planned weeks of travelling. Looking back, I am amazed that I still managed to function on this practical level. I continued to travel: flying on to Vancouver, Canada, via Los Angeles airport, where I checked in my hand baggage by mistake whilst in transit and, later, discovered items had been stolen from it. This added to my panic-stricken state and my fear that I had lost control of my safety. Friends of friends, who I arranged to meet with shortly after I arrived in Vancouver, had never met me before but could see I wasn't well. One, J, took me into her home after I'd struggled trying to cope for a week in a city-centre backpackers' hostel. I had been awake virtually all night, every night, in a heightened state of terror, and during the days I was vacantly sitting in the hostel lounge or walking and standing aimlessly in the nearby streets and was more vulnerable than I was able to realise. By now I was experiencing psychosis: the conifer trees in Stanley Park were bending over in mourning for the sad state I was causing everyone to be in; by my presence, I was contaminating good people with my evilness and making bad things happen; I received messages from the Thunderbird Totem pole in the park and any words I read on notices took on sinister twists in my mind. Everything was spiralling out of control.

After two months in Canada, my longstanding plan had been to meet up with a friend I'd previously worked with in Wales. She was scheduled to arrive in Vancouver for a final trip to Vancouver Island and a Rockies tour, before returning home together. This friend had been widowed very suddenly the year before, this was her first big holiday since and I really didn't want to let her down. Once again, my sense of duty and responsibility for others was overriding my concern for myself. When I expressed just a little of my state to my family, my mother decided to fly out for a week to try to help me stay on track for my friend's arrival. Although I was hiding the constant terrifying experiences I was having as much as possible, it was obvious I was not well and she took me to a doctor who prescribed an antidepressant. Unfortunately, in the following couple of weeks, I stopped taking the medication in the belief that it wasn't helping me.

When my friend, who knew my personality when I was well, finally arrived and I met her at the airport, she soon began to realise how unwell I was. After only a few days of travelling together on Vancouver Island, it was obvious to her that I couldn't continue our planned trip. One cold night, in the remote coastal town of Tofino, I was pacing outside the entrance to the hotel in my night clothes with bare feet. Another day, I was almost hysterical with worry; pacing at the harbour for several hours whilst my friend went on a whale watching trip as I believed that I was going to be the cause of a terrible boat accident. On the all-day coach journey back across the island to the ferry, I sat with my head down and my body in a state of rigid tension, convinced I was going to cause the coach to crash. Then, as the ferry sailed into port at Vancouver, I was horrified to see the bow doors opening before we stopped, sure that I was going to cause the ferry to sink in a catastrophic disaster.

My friend relayed the situation to the kind new friend, J, who I had been staying with and courageously completed the Rockies trip without me. J took me to her doctor and I was then taken directly by ambulance to Vancouver General Hospital. J accompanied me the whole time: when I was first taken down to the finance department to register for billing (thankfully, I wasn't billed a fee as I was, effectively, sectioned), and then for many hours whilst I was initially assessed, in a seclusion room which was frighteningly like a simple prison cell, with only a bare concrete plinth in the centre to sit on and a stainless-steel toilet in the corner.

I remained in the psychiatric unit at Vancouver General for two weeks. I was sedated and so, finally, slept properly for the first time for months. I shared a simple, two-bed room with various other female patients over the period I was there. I barely registered their presence as I was sleeping a lot. I once woke in the night to find a group of people sitting around the bed of the girl beside me. I assume they were her family. Another was a loud, biker girl with many tattoos. I remember noting that the curtains were held at the window with Velcro to prevent self-harm. We had an ensuite toilet and basin, but I was escorted, when persuaded to take a shower, by a male nurse who stood outside the shower curtain. I was supposed to choose my meals from a menu every day. I didn't make any selections, but I always had a meal and sometimes a cup of 'tea' made by another patient: an older, Asian woman who would spend time at the water station preparing drinks and then serving us. A young, dark-skinned man with an orange-dyed Mohican hairstyle regularly rode the exercise bike, in his pyjamas, in the corner of the day room which all our bedrooms opened into. A middle-aged man with an English accent, whose voice I recognised from having heard him shouting for his own clothes the day we were both assessed in seclusion, argued with his wife about crossword clues in the paper, and I only ever sat curled up on a plastic lounge sofa, hugging my legs to my chest.

It was an extremely fraught time for my parents, who were liaising with the medical teams at the hospital and at home, and eventually with the insurance company and airline, seeking permission for me to be flown home. When my father travelled over and arrived at the hospital, I was curled up in a ball in the lounge, rocking and picking at my pyjamas. I was virtually mute and couldn't really comprehend that he, or anything he said, was real. I was eventually permitted to fly home under sedation with medication given to my father to administer to me during the flight – the worst nine hours of my father's life, I'm sure. I remember he virtually collapsed at Heathrow, sobbing with the relief of getting us back. I was allowed to remain in my parents' care at their home, visited that first night by my GP, and I recovered in a matter of months with the support of visits from community psychiatric nurses, medication and cognitive behavioural therapy (CBT) when I was well enough to engage. Throughout this great ordeal for them, I had the love and care of my family.

I steadily rebuilt my social and work life, and I realised from this episode that I needed to have travel companions and greater structure and purpose to my life to stay mentally well. Unfortunately, several years later, an unresolved problematic element from my past came back to affect me again, and in an even more traumatic way. The evening before I had left to travel the world, a close friend, with whom I had previously had a short-lived relationship, sent me a surprisingly curt email stating it was best that we didn't meet to say goodbye as planned and that we should never have any contact again. This hurt me deeply as I am extremely loyal to my friends, and I couldn't understand this attitude. Some time after I had recovered completely from my illness, I received a letter from this friend asking for help as he had been made homeless. Against my better judgement and the advice of my family, I accepted him and his dog into the apartment I was living in. This apartment was next door to my family's, and they had been happy with this arrangement since it meant they were able to keep a watchful eye to ensure that I was continuing to remain mentally well.

Sadly, I resumed a relationship with this man, and we married, but I was subjected continuously to coercive, controlling and abusive behaviour from him. I now consider that this partner's previous erratic and unkind behaviour towards me had likely been a significant factor in my original illness. With the support of my sister, I eventually managed to break free from him, but there was a highly stressful and sustained period of serious harassment towards me, my family and a number of friends. This resulted in a restraining order against him and further police enquiries. I had already become clinically depressed again during this relationship. As the harassment started, I developed a constant surge of adrenalin due to the fear of his alarming behaviour; the muscles in my face twitched uncontrollably, I was a nervous wreck and psychosis started again in my mind.

There was then a year of which I have no recollection. I'm almost certain this is because of the level of anxiety I was experiencing at the time. Family members have since commented that it is just as well I don't have any memories of it, as it was not a year to remember. As before, it was hoped that medications, CBT and other psychological therapies would help me to recover. Unfortunately, for nearly three years I remained seriously clinically depressed, in a high state of anxiety and again had rigid, abnormal beliefs about my influence on the world. I was afraid that I was personally responsible for significant catastrophic events such as road traffic accidents, tsunamis and floods, and was unwaveringly convinced that I had stopped the grass from growing and leaves from appearing on trees. My family were advised to make sure I didn't watch any programmes on TV which could help me foster my beliefs. Apart from my prouncements that I had 'killed the world' and that I was actually dead, I was mostly mute again and I had no motivation to do anything. I needed prompting to eat, drink and wash. Apparently, I screamed when I showered, which must have been traumatic for my brother, who spent weekdays staying with me to care for me. I wore the same clothes with no variation and had no interest in my appearance. I was encouraged to get up and out of the house every morning to walk the family dog, which

2. Rise Like a Phoenix

I did daily on autopilot. Without the assistance of my family during this time, I would have required hospitalisation again.

It was now 2014 and, greatly concerned and frustrated that I was not getting better after nearly three years of illness and inability to work, my brother eventually sought the possibility of admission for me at the Maudsley Hospital, having watched a documentary about the work they do with their patients. Meanwhile, my sister, aware that my grandmother had successfully received ECT on several occasions in the 1950s for her severe depression, considered researching the possibility that ECT might still be a treatment option. My sister was equally concerned about the effect of my illness on my entire family – especially on my parents, with my mother suffering treatment for cancer but concerned to care for me, and my father caring for her. Researching ECT on the internet, my sister found information on the National Institute for Clinical Excellence (NICE) guidelines and was particularly impressed by a 2007 TED talk by the late Dr Sherwin Nuland. Like me, he described himself as almost catatonic prior to his treatment with ECT over thirty years before. After lengthy treatment he explained his return to health as 'rising like a phoenix' – a phrase that I love.

At a meeting with me and my family, my consultant psychiatrist eventually supported my sister's suggestion of ECT, helped by the positive comments of an accompanying nurse who had witnessed its usefulness in another part of the UK that she had previously worked in. I agreed to receive ECT, relying on this encouragement – although my decision was simply based on wanting to do anything that helped me, and thereby my family, to get me out of the hell in which we were living. The situation was now compounded by the fact that my mother had been diagnosed with stage four ovarian cancer and only had a short time remaining in life.

I was assessed and considered medically fit to receive ECT treatment at one of the two clinics in our mental health trust. Thankfully this was only a ten-minute drive from home, the other clinic in the trust being a 120-mile round trip. I was treated as an outpatient twice a week. My mother accompanied me to every session. We were always greeted at the door by the friendly smile of one of the nurses, and then we sat briefly in the waiting room, which had been thoughtfully decorated, had a window with a view to the garden outside and a daytime television programme on. Sometimes there was another patient waiting for their treatment and I would feel a bit distressed seeing them also in a depressive state, sometimes with signs of self-harm.

I never usually had to wait long to be taken into the pre-treatment room to give my consent to treatment, have my blood pressure taken and answer some memory-testing questions. If I did have to wait, we were told the reason for the delay – typically because the anaesthetist had been called to another urgent duty first. I would enter the treatment room, lie on the trolley with a pillow and sheet and the team would introduce themselves. Usually, my ECT consultant was the same each time, unless he was on holiday. I must admit, I was a little apprehensive when someone else was standing in for him as I really warmed to his positive and very friendly attitude towards me. Because my head was usually full of difficult thoughts, it was quite a relief to fall into sleep when I was given the pin prick injection into my hand and counted to three with the oxygen mask placed over my face. Five minutes later, although I wasn't aware of the time, I was in recovery being asked my name and gradually waking up. I then walked to the post-recovery area after about half an hour, where my mother was waiting. We had a cup of tea and I devoured a piece of toast since I hadn't been allowed any breakfast due to having a general anaesthetic.

My mother drove me home and I then spent a couple of hours in bed. The initial sessions left me more sleepy than subsequent ones and I had a muzzy headache sometimes. After the first few treatments, I noticed I lost a lot of the anxious feelings, but I didn't really feel any appreciable difference in my mood. I have learned since that the average number of treatments a patient receives before they get well is eight. I continued to receive my treatment twice a week (prescribed by my consultant psychiatrist) until I had had seventeen sessions and, at that point, my ECT consultant had to discuss whether it was worth continuing any longer. Typically, up to twelve sessions are prescribed, but this isn't necessarily a point to stop for some patients. With his many years of experience, my ECT consultant felt that it was worth continuing to treat me for a bit longer, in the hope that I would improve. I am so thankful that his experience was borne out by my turning a corner. After twenty-three sessions, I felt quite a difference in my mood and said that I didn't think I needed any more sessions. I wasn't instantly completely well again, but I had started to regain pleasure in activities, take more interest in my appearance again, make conversation and, very importantly to me, began to feel emotions again. At this point I was able to start moving forwards with life. I returned to work after a few months, back to a school where I volunteered to listen to children read. By the start of the next year, six months after my ECT treatment finished, I was employed full time in this busy mainstream primary school as a 1:1 teaching assistant for an autistic child, and I remained there for four happy and fun years.

Since then, I have continued to flourish and enjoy life to the full. I did not require maintenance ECT and have not had a relapse since. I will always be taking an antidepressant medication as a preventative measure, as advised by my consultant psychiatrist, but this is fine for me. My mother had been determined to care for me through my illness despite her own cancer diagnosis, extreme treatment regime and very poor terminal prognosis. She told me it was what a mother does for their child, but I know that not all mothers have this capacity. As a 'thank you' for all the care she had given me, I treated her to the trip of a lifetime together the year after I recovered and whilst she was in a period of relatively good health in remission. She had always dreamed of visiting St

Petersburg in the winter, and we spent a magical five snowy days there. After the incredibly sad death of my mother, I talked with my aunt, my mother's sister, about revisiting my childhood home in Argentina with her – something I had always wanted to do – and it led to me meeting my now husband there. Together we are now enjoying sharing life's adventures. My friends and family described my recovery as a miracle, and I feel that I was given my life back.

Although I had some temporary memory difficulties during, and for some time after, my treatment, I don't believe my cognitive function was subsequently permanently impaired and I progressed back to full-time work in education in a busy school within six months of finishing my ECT treatment. I did struggle for a few months with my autobiographical memory – my father helped me to recover this with conversations to remind me of my education and work history. I also found it difficult to put names to a number of faces I recognised and to recall geographical routes that had previously been familiar until I walked or drove them again and then it was fine. I also had some difficulty navigating my computer and the remote control for my TV, but I was also out of practice with this as I hadn't worked with them for three years. I have since studied for, and gained, my master's degree, and I work full time as a specialist tutor with students ranging from age seven at school to adults in higher education.

I was very fortunate that I was surrounded by such supportive people during my periods of severe illness – family, friends and professional teams – and I had a very positive experience of ECT. When I met my ECT consultant again, a few months after I had made a complete recovery, he was struck by my transformation and commented that he and his team hadn't realised at the time of my treatment just how ill I was.

I know that ECT continues to be perceived by many, including in the media, as an outdated and controversial treatment. In part, this is because its use in the UK is not widely discussed, it is only used for a small number of specific cases deemed suitable and how it works cannot be fully explained. Unfortunately, ECT also does not help all patients who are treated with it. However, I shudder to think what my life would be like now if I hadn't received treatment. Interestingly, a number of my medical team in Vancouver commented to my father, when I was there, that their treatment of choice, in cases of severe depression, would be ECT. I am aware that I have a higher-than-average possibility of a relapse, and I have formalised my request that ECT be the option of first choice, should I need treatment for severe depression again.

Since my treatment, I have followed Sherwin Nuland's lead and have talked about my ECT experience publicly so that others may learn from it. I have made a podcast, talked on radio and to community groups, been invited to join my ECT consultant in online medical student training and psychiatrist specialist group sessions and presented at conferences of ECT nurses. I worked as a peer reviewer for the Royal College of Psychiatrists' ECT Accreditation Service (ECTAS) as part of a team visiting UK ECT clinics to review their meeting of over 200 standards required for accreditation. I am very keen to share my experience widely in the belief that demystifying ECT is a crucial part for it to continue to be available as a treatment option.

My childhood love of the natural world has been a constant thread through my life. Whilst in my worst moments of psychosis I was convinced I had been a destructive force against nature, in my well state I know that nature is deeply healing for me. I have shared this insight whilst I worked with ECTAS and in several projects I have joined as a person with lived experience in my local mental health trust in the past few years. During the year for which I have no real memories, in the middle of my second period of depression, friends took me for a walk up a local hill which is partly covered in woodland. The only distinct memory of anything that entire year is of the sun shining on the bluebell glade we walked into at the top of the hill.

3

'Young Men Don't Need ECT'
CJ's Story

3. 'Young Men Don't Need ECT'

Backstory

I am thirty years old. From a very early age – in fact, as early as I can remember – I was aware that many of the adults in my life thought there was something not quite right about me. My childhood and teenage years were marred by abuse and trauma – a start in life which has, at many times, offered an easy explanation to those I have sought help from for the poor mental health I have experienced most of my life.

My mother left our family home in London when I was around six years old, and my two teenage sisters and I remained with my father, who worked as a handyman. Being at the younger end of the millennial generation, I enjoyed playing outside with local friends and playing video games. My family and school lives were much more complicated and, as I grew up, I remember feeling increasingly unhappy. I would often get into trouble with authority figures – particularly my father, who took a no-nonsense approach to parenting. The teaching and support staff at my primary school were so concerned about my behaviour that I had an assessment for autism, but this diagnosis was ruled out.

From the age of around six or seven, I became the victim of harmful sexual behaviour perpetrated by an adolescent for a period of over two years. After I made a difficult disclosure of this abuse to my family, my mental health began to spiral out of control. At the age of twelve, I took an overdose of over-the-counter drugs which were in my home medicine cabinet. My emotions and behaviour began to command the attention of not only my parents and school, but now also CAMHS (Child and Adolescent Mental Health Service) and social services. I was recommended an antidepressant and I can vividly recall my father flat-out refusing to agree to this in one of the many meetings we had with my psychiatrist.

At the age of twelve, I came out as gay and began talking with a man on the internet who groomed me for sexual exploitation. I remember feeling desperate for someone to love, care for and appreciate me, having endured many deeply traumatising experiences at the hands of abusive men for the trade-off of being wanted by them. At this time, I was abusing illegal drugs, truanting and was frequently going missing.

I was placed on the child protection register and later taken into care at the age of thirteen. It was not long before I was subsequently admitted into a series of CAMHS inpatient units of varying levels of security and diagnosed as having reactive attachment disorder. Between all the hospital, residential and foster care placements across England, I moved fifteen times and, on one occasion, was placed more than 200 miles from my hometown. Many of the CAMHS inpatient, residential and special school placements were chaotic and woefully inadequate environments which I believe exacerbated, rather than dealt with, the problems I faced.

With intervention and time, I got a better handle on my risky and destructive behaviour. I have the fondest memories, from the age of sixteen to eighteen, of a community CAMHS psychiatrist and psychotherapist who saw through all the destructive behaviour and who believed in my ability to move on. During this time, I had also remained in a stable foster placement following a series of placement breakdowns. CAMHS made special arrangements for me to have an inpatient detox on an adult unit at a time when there was no inpatient drug and alcohol service for young people in England. But it was not until I was seventeen years old, and I accepted a place in a therapeutic community, that I began to feel truly positive about myself and the direction my life was headed in.

After a stay of nine months in the residential therapeutic community, I left, feeling much happier and healthier, and joined a two-year outpatient group psychotherapy programme. Assessments for personality disorder were completed several times whilst I was in the therapeutic community, with the results improving as my treatment progressed. I had worked hard, with the help of others, to process the traumatic childhood I'd had, and now felt motivated to make the most of the new-found adulthood that had just started for me. Living on my own was not something I was well prepared for, but with time I began to rebuild my life, including studying at college for the GCSEs I missed out on getting in school. Living in a new part of London, relations with my family had improved, whilst at the same time I was forging new friendships through volunteering, faith and the pub.

My Worst

If we fast-forward three years to 2016, when I was twenty-one years old, I would have to say that my life at that time was the best it had ever been. I was at the end of my first year of university-level studies in Northern Ireland whilst also enjoying part-time employment utilising my lived experience to inform the work of a research centre specialising in child sexual exploitation.

I remember being exuberant, outgoing and wanting to go shopping as soon as money entered my bank account – wanting to look as good as I felt. I started to question what my life really meant and how I could be so much more than just my past and my mistakes. Developing an interest in faith and religion, I began to feel assured of the direction my life was headed. To top it all off, I had been discharged from community mental health services for over a year and was not taking any medication.

When people first discover that I have depression, they often ask what the cause or trigger was. Although the childhood trauma appears to offer a simple explanation, its impact at the onset of depression seemed to have been markedly reduced for some time and things were finally going right for me. I doubt I will ever know exactly why I stopped enjoying all the things and social company I had recently come to love, and I am also not certain of how important it is either. Pretty soon, I started to wake up every day at two or three in the morning, despite having only gone to sleep around midnight.

At first, and with encouragement from people in my life, I began to seek some help from the GP, who referred me to a primary community mental health team. I trialled taking a couple of different medications, but they made no difference, and things were fast becoming worse for me. I had a very brief, informal admission to a unit in Northern Ireland but discharged myself after one night, feeling quite triggered by memories of acute wards earlier in life.

My childhood may have been a troubled and unhappy one, but I had never experienced a depression as deep as this before. I started to hear the voices of people who had helped and advocated for me in the past, but they were now telling me how worthless and disgusting I was, belittling everything I did. My experience of the world became one where almost everything I saw, heard and thought served as proof that the only way I could make things right with God, and redeem myself for past misdeeds, was to end my life. Beginning to obsess over plans to kill myself, I came as close as placing a cord around my neck. But I was unable to tie it, and instead burst into tears.

From the beginning of the depression, I was willing to seek and accept help, at one point even being desperate for help. Later, I started shunning support. I was offered further hospital admissions on three separate occasions but refused each time, now squarely believing that the only option for me was death. Some of my psychiatric history, particularly in my teenage years, was felt to be consistent with personality disorder, and it later came to my knowledge that this was a key factor in decisions not to consider detention ('sectioning') when I refused the offers of an

3. 'Young Men Don't Need ECT'

informal (voluntary) hospital admission. I believe this may have resulted in delays in appropriate treatment for my depression.

Pretty soon, I couldn't taste anything anymore and I couldn't even cry, feeling numb and almost emotionless. It was as though my body just stopped working and there was a disconnect between my most basic needs and my motivation to meet them. I began to withdraw from the world around me, from friends and family. I would turn on the television to watch music channels, as music seemed to help me blur the voices. After a while, the people in the music videos became disapproving of me and were giving me signals that I was nothing but a troublemaker. I guess this was part of the reason for my withdrawal from my family and my friends. I just wanted to be alone; I couldn't enjoy company. I wasn't hungry for food; I wasn't using the bathroom to clean myself. People have told me since that I wasn't even making sense. I withdrew from everything.

Towards the end of 2016, I stopped eating and drinking for a prolonged period and, as a result, began to have symptoms associated with acute kidney injury. I was taken to hospital by a friend and, after a brief period of supportive care in the general hospital, I was transferred to an acute mental health ward.

During this admission I also had another assessment for personality disorder, with the rating scale used (SCID-II) showing 'multiple dysfunctional personality traits', although I was not definitively meeting the criteria for diagnosis of any personality disorder. I believe my treatment in the therapeutic community had truly adapted according to the way I thought and behaved, enabling me to move past some of the problematic ways I interacted with the world as a teenager. I know that the effects of this treatment remain to this day. It is hardly surprising that there are lasting effects of the traumatic life I experienced as a child, but what was going on at the time of this admission was markedly different from anything I had experienced before. Having effective treatment for childhood trauma, and resulting interpersonal/personality issues, does not afford immunity from depressive illness, and I think it is unhelpful when clinicians automatically assume someone with such a past is only suitable for treatments for personality disorder when their mental health declines, as mine did.

ECT Begins

I do not have the clearest memories of being offered ECT, but I remember being told that it was considered to be the best treatment for my condition and I was asked to agree to it. Although I gave my consent to the treatment without any objection, I was not convinced it would work. Still feeling committed to ending my life, I had been scanning the ward environment for ways to do so.

ECT was very effective for me in the short term, and I felt noticeably better after the first three treatments. I started to feel motivated to address how I had neglected myself and was allowed to have a shave under supervision. I also reached out to a friend and later had visits from them, as well as from my university lecturer, who brought in a laptop for me to catch up on my assignments.

Whilst trying to be cautious about how fast this was all happening, I couldn't help but want to discontinue ECT and leave hospital, given how much better I felt. The ward consultant and nurses seemed to agree, and I was discharged after just three months on the ward and told I could go back to work and resume my studies.

First Relapse: Rio de Janeiro

Although ECT brought rather quick relief from the depression, this did not last and my mood began to decline around a month after I had been discharged. The community mental health team adjusted my medication, and I continued to monitor the situation, but a hospital admission or more ECT was not on my mind at this point as I remained highly functional and motivated to get on with life.

About two months after I was discharged from hospital and stopped having ECT, I travelled to Rio de Janeiro with my manager and colleagues to present at an international research conference. Whilst there, I began to feel very low, especially in the mornings, and I started to hear voices again, although this time I was aware I was experiencing hallucinations.

It was agreed that I needed to return home on an earlier flight, but the travel insurer insisted on a psychiatric assessment to provide confirmation that I was well enough for air travel. The outcome of that assessment resulted in me being admitted to an inpatient private mental health clinic at the assessing psychiatrist's insistence.

The consultant at the clinic arranged for me to quickly restart ECT within the first week or two of the admission; she said she believed I did not have 'enough' ECT sessions the first time. I was impressed by how promptly she recognised that ECT had been effective for me in the past and that a quick recovery was important so that my return home was not unnecessarily delayed. This experience felt like the total opposite of the gatekeeping of ECT I have often experienced in the UK. Having treatment three times per week, I began improving even faster than the last time and was discharged after five weeks from the clinic. After I had recovered and was speaking to the psychiatrist about how difficult it can be to access ECT in the UK, I remember making a sarcastic comment that 'it would be more than worth the cost of the plane ticket to have all my breakdowns in Brazil'.

The clinic recommended maintenance ECT going forward, but I was told by the NHS community mental health team when I got returned to the UK that 'maintenance ECT is not recommended in NICE guidelines' and that it would therefore not be offered.

Second Relapse

Approximately 3 months after I got back to the UK, I relapsed again and was admitted to yet another acute ward. The consultant on this ward was especially keen to avoid using ECT again even though I was requesting it because nothing else had worked thus far. I began to get very frustrated, feeling like I was not being listened to. Because of severe bed shortages for mental health patients across Northern Ireland, I was admitted to a ward intended for older people, despite being only twenty-three years old. There was an older female patient on the ward having ECT and I formed an impression that assumptions were being made that, because I was a young man, ECT was not a suitable treatment for me.

Feeling increasingly frustrated and desperate, I tied my shoelaces around my neck and anchored it around a bed curtain rail, which collapsed to the ground when I jumped. I was placed on 1:1 nursing observation, which meant I had a nurse supervise me at all times, including when using the bathroom. I had a further, ineffective trial of another antidepressant, a change in antipsychotic and lithium augmentation, being told that it would be better if an effective drug treatment could be found rather than repeating ECT again. It was nearly three months before I was finally offered a course of ECT. Afterwards, my request for maintenance was once again brushed off with the insistence that 'it was not Trust policy to offer maintenance ECT as it is not supported by NICE guidelines'.

During the admission, I had yet another assessment for personality disorder. When I am severely depressed, I often do not think or behave as rationally as I would otherwise. Clinicians who have only ever seen me in this state may confuse this for ingrained patterns of behaviour and thought, subsequently affecting the treatment I am offered (or not offered). It seemed my word about what problems I was facing, and what had helped in the past, was not good enough for the treating psychiatrist.

After this admission, my three years of studies had become so disrupted by periods of ill health that continuation of my academic course was no longer viable. I therefore abandoned my studies in Northern Ireland and returned to London to live there permanently. I felt very disappointed that this happened, especially given that I had achieved so highly in the work I had submitted.

Third Relapse

It wasn't long before I became depressed again. I knew that I was getting unwell. In the past, when I was hearing voices, I didn't realise they were not real. In later years I became aware they were not real, although they always sounded very real to me; for example, I could recognise who was talking to me. On this occasion, I started hearing voices again and realised that the depression was coming back. I decided to contact a crisis line for patients so I didn't have to worry my friends and relatives, as I had done on previous occasions. The person at the other end of the line told me that I should go to A&E, which resulted in me being referred to the home treatment team. However, I felt that this team, and the consultant in charge, did not realise that my condition was serious. Once again, my suggestion that I needed ECT was dismissed. Eventually, my situation became unmanageable: I was thinking of killing myself all the time, as I was getting sick of the cycle of relapses. During one brief admission to hospital, I drank some detergent. Over the course of a few days, I had accumulated a decent amount of laundry washing liquid by pretending to go to the laundry several times and obtaining a small amount in plastic cups on each occasion, from different members of staff. However, it turned out that this liquid is specially chosen by hospitals as being less toxic, precisely to prevent such events. I felt sick but was unharmed. Finally, I was detained under the Mental Health Act and was admitted to a hospital in London. This time I was offered

ECT and, as they knew that I had wanted this treatment in the past, I was able to sign a consent form. Before I signed the form, I asked what would happen after I became well again. On this occasion the ward consultant told me that I would continue with maintenance ECT. I was discharged in June 2018, and received maintenance ECT, which I am still currently having more than six years later.

Life on Maintenance

Although I still live with the ups and downs of chronic depression in my daily life, I've been much more stable recently, and have not had an inpatient admission to an acute mental health ward since the commencement of maintenance ECT. I was also referred to the National Affective Disorders Service, which specialises in complex and treatment-resistant depression. They recommended that I have implanted vagus nerve stimulation, a minimally invasive surgical procedure. Whilst the process of obtaining NHS funding authorisation can be difficult and complex, I am hopeful that this treatment could offer further relief for me from depression.

It's been a long journey and has felt like a fight – not only to get the ECT treatment in the first place, but to be given the opportunity to have, what I believe to be, crucial maintenance ECT. I now have ECT every five weeks and the stability that this has afforded me means that I have been able to resume my studies.

In the past I had excelled academically, but my illness prevented me from completing a degree. Shortly after the maintenance ECT began, I started a degree (a BSc in Health and Social Care), studying full time. I was also well enough to resume working part time as a research assistant at a UK university. This year, I have been accepted into the University of Oxford to do a two-year research master's degree, working towards a PhD. This is huge, and I am very proud to have progressed so far in what I love doing.

Of course, I feel scared and nervous because of the intensive nature of the academic requirements, never mind the pressure that comes with the prestige of this being Oxford! But I've been in touch with their student support team, and they have been excellent in accommodating my needs.

I continue to live with depression, which can be debilitating. Every time I get the maintenance ECT session, I'm acutely aware that the positive effect it has won't last and, like a sand timer, my improved mood will run out eventually and I'll need more treatment.

But I will embrace what Oxford brings, and, coming from a social housing estate background, I am actually looking forward to attending the formal dinners and meeting and mixing with people from all walks of life!

I'd like to share one last thing: a recent event that happened to me and which has had the most profound impact. I was experiencing troubling symptoms which I was concerned could be indicative of cancer. I remember beginning to sob rather powerfully after I ended the call to my doctor's surgery to make an appointment. I was starting to think how unfair and tragic it would be if I was now going to die after only just beginning to feel alive again. Before I left for my appointment, I received the email I had been anxiously waiting several months for – the decision on my application for a scholarship for my place at Oxford. I had been awarded a generous scholarship yet, given my overarching concern about my health and fate, I felt a sense of cruelty rather than celebration. Falling into a profound desperation, I began to open my heart in a tearful prayer about how much I now wanted to live despite years of wanting (and indeed trying) to die.

But then I felt both relieved and a bit silly after the doctor reassured me that I only had a urinary tract infection. After

I arrived home, I began to marvel at the profound progression of mindset that had developed from wanting to die to wanting to live. I may have stopped wanting to kill myself some time ago, but I still believed I was only ambivalent about continuing to live whilst, at the same time, seeking opportunities to advance in almost every area of my life. I see now that, far from being ambivalent about continuing my life, I have committed myself to doing so.

4

Back from the Edge
Karen's Story

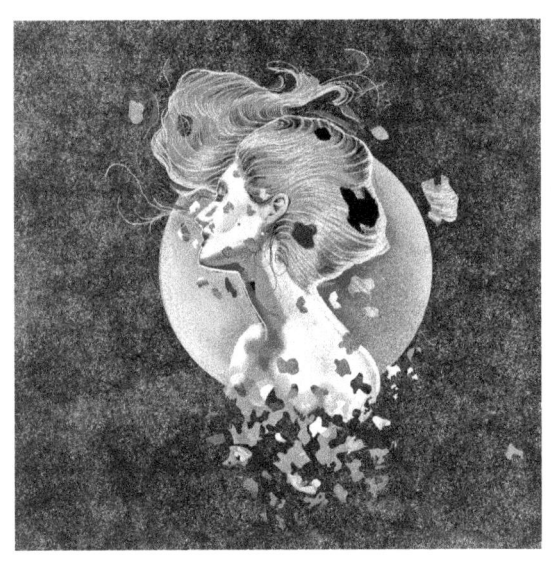

It

Uninvited *It* enters and with awful persistence
It slowly erodes all your strength and resistance
A parasite that feeds on the innermost you
It gets stronger and stronger whatever you do
It laughs at your weakness and bathes in your tears
It pours negativity into your ears
Removing happy and hopeful *It* places instead
Sadness and despair deep into your head
It builds a glass wall that separates you
From the world all around and the things that they do
It takes all of the colours and meanings away
The darkness of night replaces the day
It grips you so hard and drains you from you
Till there's just a shell left but *It* wants that too
It takes hold of your hand to show you the way
There is the void, will you jump in or stay?

(10th December 2009)

To those looking in on my life, to all intents and purposes I look fairly 'normal'. I work, participate wholeheartedly in a busy family life and I'm physically active. I enjoy life and all that it brings, but it hasn't always been this way.

In 2009, I visited my GP as I recognised that my mood had dropped: I had lost my sense of purpose and enjoyment of life. There had been some major events and changes in our family in the preceding few years, including the sudden death of my father-in-law, a large financial fraud conducted against us that involved threats of violence, and my youngest son's ongoing health problems. These culminated in my husband (P) being diagnosed with a serious health condition with a poor prognosis, which meant I had to leave work and become his carer. There did come a point where things started to resolve, but I began to struggle ...

Following discussion with my GP, we decided my low mood was an understandable reaction to the circumstances and stresses of the previous few years and I began to see the practice counsellor to talk it through. After a few months, the counsellor became concerned that my mood was still dropping and, after further discussion, I started on an antidepressant. Despite continuing to see the counsellor, regular appointments with my GP and the medication, my mental health continued to decline and I became increasingly unwell. I was referred to the community mental health team, my medication was changed and my mood began to improve.

Unfortunately, the improvement didn't last and my mood dropped again. I also became anxious and withdrawn and lost weight. I felt overwhelmed, unable to cope with day-to-day family life and started to have suicidal thoughts.

Diary Entry 30th October 2009
Why can't I just feel better again? I am taking the tablets, having the counselling, and really trying to explore my feelings and get it straight in my head. I get a couple of days when things seem ok but then I hit the bottom again. Is this how it's going to be? If the ok feelings aren't going to stay, then I can't do it. I am no good to anyone like this. The last few days I have even turned away from C when he has come to me for a hug, what sort of mum am I, turning away a six-year-old?

Diary Entry 30th October 2009
Numb, but not numb enough. Would they be better off without me? I think maybe they would. I am scared of where these feelings are taking me to. Don't really feel anything, just bad. Can't see how this will pan out, can't see anything. Feel like I am staring into a big black hole, there is nothing there.

Diary Entry 16th November 2009
Feel like I am watching myself doing things, I can see what I'm doing, and I know I am doing it, but I am not connected to it. Think maybe I am going totally mad, nothing feels right.

Diary Entry 23rd November 2009
Don't want to talk to anyone or even be near them. I'm not part of their world and I don't have the energy to get back to it. I can't eat, I'm just living on fresh air and coffee. I don't know who I am or where I am, I have lost myself. I may as well be gone forever because this is unbearable. P is scared but I cannot reassure him that it will be ok, feel like I am sinking and I'm already too far in to get back out again.

Diary Entry 27th November 2009
I don't want anyone to see me, I am deeply ashamed of myself, why can't I cope? Something deep inside me is fundamentally bad and I can't hide it anymore. I think I am lost forever; I don't even know where to start looking or even if I want to. Just want out of it, I can't be in this empty colourless shell. I am no use to anyone and I'm just causing too much pain to them all. I can't be here anymore. If I could get the tablets, I know what to take. I don't know where P has hidden them, but I need to find them.

Diary Entry 30th November 2009
I am dead inside, there is no point being here, please let it end. The feeling that I shouldn't be here is overwhelming. Never has something that should be wrong felt so right. I have come to the end, I can go no further I don't want this life.

Following this, I was admitted to hospital where I stayed for six weeks and stabilised on a new medication.

I stayed well for a couple of months, but things gradually started to slip back again and I was readmitted to hospital.

Diary Entry 29th March 2010
The last few days have passed in a confused blur. Seems like I have been here forever, I have lost track of time and I feel detached from it all. They keep trying to make me eat but I need to feel hollow and empty, then my head will be hollow and empty. I am in my own mad sad world. The doctor came to see me, he knows the not eating

is part of something else. If you don't talk about it, does that mean you can say it didn't happen? If you talk about it, does that mean it is real?

At this point I disclosed to my psychiatrist that, thirty years previously, when I was fourteen, I had been raped by a stranger on my way home from a friend's house but had never told anyone about it or ever acknowledged it to myself. I was diagnosed with major depressive disorder and post-traumatic stress disorder (PTSD) and my life imploded.

William Styron, an American novelist and essayist, wrote in his autobiographical work *Darkness Visible: A Memoir of Madness*:

> Depression is a word that has slithered innocuously through the language like a slug, leaving little trace of its intrinsic malevolence and preventing by its very insipidity, a general awareness of the horrible intensity of the disease when out of control.

I can completely relate to this quote and the utter inadequacy of the word 'depression' to describe what it is; for me, my depression, and the effects of it, became out of control.

I tried to pursue counselling with a specialist counsellor from a local rape crisis centre, but my mood became so low I stopped eating completely, did not look after myself, did not talk and began to self-harm. I couldn't engage with the counselling and became actively suicidal. My family were terrified for my safety and at a loss for how to help.

Diary Entry 5th May 2010
There isn't an end is there – only if I make it myself.

I attempted suicide and was sectioned. Again, my medication was changed, but there was little improvement.

This Feeling
I can't stand this feeling I want it to go
But it remains defiant, refuses, says no

I can't talk it away or chase off with tears
I do both of these things but it still reappears
Invisible bonds attach it to me
I wish I could break them I want to be free
It's deep and dark, intense and so strong
It makes everything else seem so very wrong
This feeling exhausts me drains everything out
I no longer remember what life is about

(1st October 2010)

Diary Entry 2nd October 2010

I am not sure if this is really happening – what if it is a dream and not real? You say you understand but how can you understand me when I can't understand myself? Whose life is this because it's not mine?

Diary Entry 4th October 2010

Would I do it again if I had the chance? Yes, yes, yes. The nurse says I would not get very far if I ran but I am desperate to run, it's all building up again. Please do something to make it all stop, you have taken all my choices away but not given me anything in return, only wait and it will get better but how much longer?

Diary Entry 7th October 2010

More new medication. I hate it here what a total f***ing mess all this is. Why can't I choose my own path in life, even if that is death? Let me out, I can't breathe. Maybe I should make that real. There is no happy ever after. Is there a happy anything?

Diary Entry 11th October 2010

Tried not to breathe. Have had all belts and cords removed. My very limited choices are now even more limited and I have a nurse within touching distance in my room. I love them but I hate myself more. This is torture. Medication is being increased again.

4. Back from the Edge

Diary Entry 19th November 2010
???ECT WTF???

I was vaguely aware of what ECT was when it was suggested to me and my family, from my nurse training many years before, but I had no real knowledge about it. It sounded terrifying but so did continuing to exist as I was, and so I decided to have the treatment. At the end of 2010 I had my first course of ECT. People around me noticed an improvement after a couple of treatments, but it took a couple more until I became aware of a change myself. I began to eat and drink and speak again and my mood lifted so I was no longer suicidal, and I was discharged.

Diary Entry 3rd December 2010
3rd session of ECT. Have bad headache and shaky and feel a bit strange. Slept for ages. I really hope this works; I don't want all this for nothing. People say I seem different, but I don't feel it.

Diary Entry 7th December 2010
More ECT again. Have awful head and shaky. Apparently had a long fit again. Asleep for a long time, lots of paracetamol. No visitors today and I am missing everyone, but they are coming tomorrow and it will be good to see them. I think I might ask them to bring me something to eat.

Diary Entry 20th April 2011
I am feeling better and have decided to start writing my diary again. I have books covering my numerous times in hospital, suicide attempts and being sectioned, ECT and outpatients' visits. Even when I read them, I still can't remember what happened very clearly, thank you ECT, not sure my memory and losing words will get much better to be honest. So here I am trying to recover from major depressive disorder, PTSD flashbacks, getting zapped and heavy-duty medication. Not

sure if I can recover from this but I know I have to try – there is too much to lose. I've started to see J at the rape crisis centre, the sessions are really, really hard but I absolutely have to do them.

Diary Entry 4th May 2011
Don't feel very good today. It was the Royal Wedding street party and I managed to go but was so anxious. Sometimes I think I am doing ok and can cope with stuff, then I think I just can't do this. Meds still causing problems but if they are changed again, I may slip further back. I think I need help, it's so hard.

Diary Entry 3rd June 2011
Back on the ward again. Didn't see that coming. I thought I was on the edge of the hole but no, I'm back in it again. How, how, how? Took a box of the little blue tablets that are usually my friend, and ended up in A&E. I remember none of it. I'm not sectioned thank God, but I have to stay or I will be. Have disappointed P and everyone else. Miss them all and I can't bear how upset C was. They are changing my medication and may consider ECT again. My life is a major mess and I don't know how to untangle it. I have done all that is asked of me (apart from the overdose). I have taken the tablets that are now being altered all over the place. I talk, I try not to engage in unhelpful behaviours, but it is still never enough. Why and will it ever be? I can't be like this; I don't know who this person is, but it is not me.

Diary Entry 9th June 2011
Doctors have decided against ECT at present but have prescribed a small dose of antipsychotic drugs alongside the medication change. I am to stop seeing J at the rape crisis centre – I hate this idea – but I have been referred to a psychologist for EMDR therapy, whatever that is and whenever it happens.

Diary Entry 2nd August 2011
Appointment with the psychologist, she says I definitely have PTSD and all my symptoms are classic, it's not just me. She has given me 4

initial appointments to make sure it's the right route. If it's not, then what? They stopped me seeing J. Doctors are happy that the new regime of meds seems to have settled down and will hopefully do what it is intended to. I can go home tomorrow!

Following this discharge, I had a few months of relative stability. We had a family holiday, I made an action plan of things I wanted to achieve and how to achieve them, my family and friends were very supportive and encouraging, I kept taking my medication and I started the EMDR sessions with the psychologist. However, as we got further into it, my mood began to deteriorate again, and by December things became intolerable.

No Escape

When I open my eyes disappointment I feel
The world is still there and still all so real
My wish is to sleep and never awake
If I had that choice it is one I would take
That choice is not an option for me
No easy release no chance to be free
I must stay here and suffer unbearable pain
To suffer this punishment here I remain
They say I'll feel better this darkness will lift
But I've spent too long already waiting for it to shift
Torment in my head there's a battle inside
Bad thoughts and feelings crash and collide
How can it be better for me to stay?
When each day I still suffer in this awful way
I look at the photos – even they're not enough
I feel guilt shame and worthlessness a host of bad stuff
Even for them I can't battle on
My connections to them broken and gone
I question just how I came to be here
But there are no answers only the fear
That I'll never be able to get away
From the unending pain – I'll be forced to stay

(18th December 2011)

Diary Entry 11th January 2012

I suppose what was inevitable has happened: back on the ward. On a 72-hour section on level 1, with someone watching me all the time. Everyone says tell the truth but that's not going to get me very far. What a rubbish piss-poor excuse for a mother and human being I am. I would truly be better off gone and so would everyone else. My options are very limited – they took the tablets in the bag and strip searched me for the others. All cords and wires gone and I can't get out. I have something I found in my holdall that they didn't, but apart from that, I don't know. Feel really calm about it, but know I have to do it as I can't bear this any longer. I can't get him away from me whatever I do, he is there. I know it will mean he has won, but at least I won't have to be near him. Then I am left with what will I do to them but what the hell am I doing to them now? I must write them a letter and explain why and make sure they know that, above all, I love them.

3pm

They have put me on a section 3. Not sure how long that lasts, will have to ask. Ruining everyone's life and making it so much harder again. Feel very disorientated and detached. How the hell did this happen again? Don't want it, don't want anything.

10.15pm

The section lasts 6 months. WTF have I done? This cannot be happening, but it is. Everyone will hate me even more than they already do. I want to go home. I want to lose myself forever. Have I lost my chance with the psychologist because that would be a disaster? Am I ever going to get better because I can't see it? The nurse in my room told me to think about my kids, but I do think about them and, believe me, I need no prompting to feel guilty about them.

4. Back from the Edge

Diary Entry 13th January 2012

Friday the 13th but it can't get much worse. Not eaten since Monday, maybe this will help me get where I want to be. Just spoke to C, I ruined his 9th birthday and can't stop crying at the enormity of the situation. What a shit excuse for a mother I am. This whole thing would be better off finished asap. Why won't they just let me do it? I don't want to be here with the guilt, pain, badness, etc. It's all too difficult. Just let me go. I have made such a mess of it all, where's me gone and who is me anyway?

Diary Entry 15th January 2012

They say I'm here for my own safety, but I don't want to be safe. Now is when my plans need to work.

Diary Entry 17th January 2012

I tried but they found me too soon. They are talking about ECT again. P says to have it as it worked before, as do most of the other people I've talked to, so maybe that is the way to go.

Diary Entry 19th January 2012

Ward round today. I am to have more ECT next week and a change of meds. It will be a quick changeover so I will feel horrible for a few days which, combined with the ECT, will be a whole lot of fun. I feel so sad as C didn't ring to say goodnight and am stupidly upset. I don't feel like part of their lives at the moment, any of them. I have lost my identity as a mum, I hate it. Not looking forward to the next few days/weeks. None of this is right. I am missing so much of life. This is NOT a life.

Diary Entry 20th January 2012

Signed all the ECT papers today and will be having the first one on Monday. I'm really scared about it now. What if I have it and it doesn't work or makes me worse? How can it not be doing damage, what if I forget everything? It did make me feel better before but it feels like a risk, but one I don't have much choice about if I want to be better . . .

Diary Entry 24th January 2012
Yesterday was hideous. Felt the worst that I have out of all the ECTs and I wet myself. Headache still this morning, legs aching and teeth hurting. Nurse told me I had to have more anaesthetic to keep me asleep for longer because the fit lasted a long time. Not looking forward to 6-12 of these. Just need to sleep.

Diary Entry 26th January 2012
ECT day. Must have been a shorter fit because awake much quicker and with less headache but I think they said a longer fit is supposed to be best. Just want to be better. How am I ever going to get out of here and what if this is my life now? What am I doing to C and everyone else? I don't want this. I still have my security blanket: yes or no?

Diary Entry 29th January 2012
P, B and C came to see me and I want their lives to go on around me, but I'm moving further and further away, as though I don't belong with them anymore. Still thinking they are better off without me. I need to set them free - free from me. I'm drifting away from them and this could be the time I never drift back.

Diary Entry 30th January 2012
3rd ECT today - headache and knocked out. Meds changed again. Off level 1, no one in my room watching me. This is not fair on anyone. It cannot carry on.

Diary Entry 1st February 2012
And so begins another month. Wish I knew what was going to happen. Please tell me I don't belong here. I want to go back to the normal world, but normal people don't get their brains fried. Normal people have a life. P and C came later, I wonder how all this affects C and I miss them so much.

Diary Entry 2nd February 2012
ECT day. One flew over the cuckoo's nest and I'm in it. Got to fight somehow. He's had me once he can't take me forever.

Diary Entry 6th February 2012
ECT number 5. Really shit headache, took quite a long time to come around. This has to work. I just want to be better.

Diary Entry 10th February 2012
ECT day. Head really horrible. Just coming round properly at 4.30pm. Doctor says 2 more, then assess. Sometimes I think I feel a bit better and sometimes I'm still so low. This place and the changes in meds don't help. I just want to be better. Everybody is having a family meal on Sunday – something else I will miss.

Diary Entry 15th February 2012
7th ECT yesterday. Head horrible but people say I look brighter today, but need to assess how I feel, that's the hard part. Feel like everything is up in the air and could fall anywhere.

Diary Entry 17th February 2012
ECT number 8. Head killing and aching – grim.

Diary Entry 18th February 2012
I think I feel a bit better today, please please let the ECT be having some effect. Might be starting to see the psychologist again next week. Please let things be starting to move properly. I'm seeing them all tomorrow and that will be so good.

Diary Entry 21st February 2012
ECT number 9. Took quite a while to come round from it again today. Feeling a bit brighter at the moment, I just hope it can grow from here.

Diary Entry 24th February 2012
Had number 10 ECT. Now only one more week to go then I don't know what next. Psychologist came yesterday and we started the work again, which is good.

Diary Entry 1st March 2012
Ward round – I am to finish the course of 12 ECTs, number 12 tomorrow. I can have some leave at the weekend, first time out of this place for months.

I remained on the ward under a section and began the trauma work with the psychologist. The work was very difficult and, as we explored what had happened, more details returned to my memory. It seemed that, as my mood had become better, the PTSD became worse, with daily flashbacks and nightmares. Throughout March, I became increasingly desperate again, and attempted suicide on two occasions. Home leave stopped and I was put back onto level 1 again. My memories of the time are of being distraught and exhausted with a constant battle going on with myself to find ways to make it end permanently, and being unable to convey adequately the distress I was feeling. Each ward round, I would beg the doctor to let me die, only to be told, again, they would not let that happen. I was on big doses of benzodiazepines, sleeping tablets and extra olanzapine to try to keep me blunted whilst tackling the PTSD.

Diary Entry 26th March 2012
Ward round – Flashback in the middle of the session. Doctor says my distress is very plain for all to see and can understand my desperation, but I will be kept safe 24/7. Night-time olanzapine doubled to 10mg which should have a very sedating effect combined with the temazepam and I will get some sleep. Can still have when required dose if needed and lorazepam. He is going to talk to the psychologist to work out a plan but I will not

4. Back from the Edge

be allowed to kill myself. Going to take a long time. He is positive I will get there but he is concerned about how ill I am. I'm just exhausted and I want it to end. I have no fight left and don't even want to fight it. Who am I – me now 46 or me 14? What to do apart from die. The tablets don't help me sleep so I'm going to save them up.

Blackness

Down in the darkness cocooned in the black
Really can't see that there's any way back
Sinking right under gasping for air
Knowing it's real it is not a nightmare
Don't want to be reached, don't want to be saved
Let me just be a shadow to show where I've laid
I'll succumb to the darkness let it flow through my veins
Embrace all the nothingness the blackness contains
My head will not think and my eyes will not see
What I was will be gone I just want to be free
I just want to go I cannot stay here
Everything's calm and so very clear
The place where I'll go will have nothing of you
Your face will be blocked and the things you did too
To get there's a struggle but to stay even more
The blackness is something that is worth fighting for
I've let you destroy me, followed you to this place
What I was or what I could be disappeared with no trace

(1st April 2012)

Diary Entry 16th April 2012

Saw psychologist. She said we cannot work together at the moment because the therapy is not helping and I am still suicidal. Going over things again and again and making it worse. Maybe when I am 'more stable and safe' we can begin again? Says I have to stop seeing him as the big bad wolf, he was just a man, inadequate and sick, and I was in the wrong place at the wrong time, it could have been anyone. I need to be angry with him and not turn that anger inwards. I have failed. This was one of my big hopes to help me get better. Now what? How am I going to get stable and safe?

Diary Entry 17th April 2012
Today is the day 32 years ago. What else can I say? Just want to curl up and die. How can I get through this now I have been dropped by the psychologist? What to do? Told my nurse, she didn't know. She says we can make a new plan forward and I am a survivor. So why don't I feel like one? Doctor has written me a dose of olanzapine today, I need to be out of it and numb. Being kept safe but I don't want to be safe. Had a room search and they found what I was hiding.

Diary Entry 19th April 2012
Ward round – meds adjusted. The doctor is referring me to G, another psychologist who specialises in PTSD through CBT (cognitive behavioural therapy) but says I need a few weeks break from therapy, but I can work with my nurse on the ward.

Diary Entry 21st April 2012
Visit from P and C. C got a bit stroppy and upset just before they left, which I hate. P very quiet, looks tired and says he isn't sleeping very well – work, kids, running the house, me ... Feel very bad as I am causing so much trouble and bound to be more to come. Always said what I would do if I caused more harm than good, but I can't even do that on a level 1 with nothing here. Why keep me safe when it would be for the good of us all if I wasn't here?

I continued to work with my nurse on the ward, my medication was changed again and, very gradually, I began to feel more in control of things. My observation levels were reduced and I started to get section 17 leave that gradually increased. I was discharged on 21st June, continuing on medication and waiting to see G, the new psychologist. I had a period of relative stability and started to work with G on trauma-focused CBT in 2013.

Diary Entry 8th May 2013

Feeling really apprehensive about tomorrow's session with G because we are doing the narrative about what happened. Last time I went through this, I ended up getting sectioned. Everyone says I am in a better place now and I really hope so because I have to do this.

Diary Entry 9th May 2013

Did the first half of the narrative – horrible, horrible. Every time I tell someone, it's like it was the first time. I don't feel any better or any relief, just shame – like I am 14 again. Did some grounding and went to my safe place. I have to stay in control.

Diary Entry 11th May 2013

Trying all the distraction techniques but it's hit or miss if it helps. Want to get the hair straighteners out. How bad is that? How stupid am I???? Haven't done it for months, can't start now. Going for a walk to get away from it. Texted P to tell him what I wanted to do so at least I haven't kept it secret. Don't want to lose myself in it.

Diary Entry 15th May 2013

Appointment with G for the second half of the narrative. Worse than last time and I feel ashamed, guilty, bad, dirty – nothing good. Trying to remember I am not 14 but it feels so raw. Went as far as putting the straighteners on to heat up, the urge to do something to get rid of all the bad feelings was overwhelming. Managed to switch them off and took a diazepam instead. I don't like this, it doesn't feel good and I am scared about losing control.

Diary Entry 18th May 2013

Spent the day in bed, bed feels safe. Feel like I am drowning in it. I don't feel clean and I don't want to be touched. Isolating myself and

I don't want people to see me. I can see the marks he left on me so they must be able to as well. This is irrational I know. G said I have to try to challenge the thought that I am bad.

Diary Entry 23rd May 2013
Stuck on repeat and I feel ambushed by it all. I have important things coming up that I mustn't ruin for everyone: A's graduation, my brother's wedding and our holiday. I feel on edge, like I'm waiting for something to happen. Found some apps for my phone to help with distraction but the lure of the straighteners is strong. Keep telling myself the pain only works for a short time and the guilt after makes me feel worse. Next door's lawnmower set off a flashback, awful physical sensations.

Diary Entry 3rd June 2013
Did the reliving with G, not sure if I can say just how horrible it was. So many thoughts and sensations and I feel quite devastated again. I have tried so hard to forget what he did for so long and it's too real now. Trying so hard to tell myself I am not 14 but it honestly feels like I am. Want those straighteners so much but went with the diazepam instead. Wonder how many it would take to reach oblivion, not forever just now.

Diary Entry 10th June 2013
Did something really, really stupid – gave in to the straighteners. I had to get him out of my head. I have let everyone down and now I have another badge of shame. When I am doing it, it feels like I'm in control, but afterwards like I have lost control. G is going to speak to the doctor and she is concerned about my safety. She told me to go and get my arm looked at and they said I need a skin graft. Why, why, why am I so stupid?

Diary Entry 21st June 2013
The longest day officially but all days seem never-ending. It plays on a loop in my head. I hate how he has so much control over me.

G says we have to stick with it and the details are needed to be able to process the memory and the anxiety levels will come down. Will it ever be ok? It has to be because I can't live with it and I can't function in any role. Can't be a mother, can't be a wife, can't be a daughter and, if I can't be any of those things, there is no point in being.

The therapy continued, the flashbacks and nightmares intensified and my mood dropped further. I have limited memories of that period, but I am able to piece events together from diaries written at the time, family and friends telling me what happened and reading my medical notes:

Diary Entry 13th August 2013
Told G I can't sleep because of the flashbacks and nightmares, I don't want to eat and my mood is dropping more. She said I have to go through this and it is a normal reaction. Questioning whether I will get through it, feels like I am falling apart. Very scared of what might happen. He won't leave me alone. Feel weird, like I am not real and am watching myself from a distance, even though I know I am real.

Diary Entry 14th August 2013
G says I have depersonalisation as a reaction to the traumatic stuff we are covering. She is concerned about no sleep and no food and my 'back-up plan'. She mentioned being admitted as a possible option so we can continue with the therapy, but I will be safe. Not sure about that. I still don't feel right, I have a funny noise in my head like whispering and I don't like it.

Diary Entry 18th August 2013
I started to hear his voice a few days ago, gradually becoming louder and more abusive. I am very scared. P sat up with me for most of the night, but he won't go away. P took me to see G and she said it is some sort of reactive psychosis to the work we are doing. She said I had no choice about being admitted and called the crisis team.

I used my back up plan and took all the tablets I had. I remember nothing until the next day. I tried to run away but there were 2 security guards at the end of my bed who stopped me several times. My doctor came with another psychiatrist and two social workers. He asked me again to agree to going in, but I refused because how can I finish it off in there? So, they sectioned me on a section 3 and I'm here stuck on a 1 to 1 watch guard. But he's here too, and a lot of the time he shouts, especially when I am asleep, to wake me up and he is watching me. I can't sleep or eat and now he has started to touch me. People keep saying he is in my head and I am ill but I know he is very real. He told me if I told anyone he would come and find me and he has. This is beyond unbearable; I have to finish it. I have a plan, just need to find the opportunity to do it. Not writing it here in case anyone finds out.

Wipe out
If I can't lose you then I'm afraid I'll lose me
I can't keep going I don't know how to be
I feel like I'm being slowly wiped out
It's hard to remember what life is about.
I wake up in the morning and I'm unable to see
The end of the day and I just want to flee
You've lived inside me uninvited for years
Now you're on the rampage and I'm living in fear
If I look in the mirror I can't see who looks back
I don't recognise me everything's black
I feel violated over and over again
And it's all too much I can't stand the pain
I can't keep doing this anymore
I feel unclean to the middle of my core
I am not strong I am just too weak
And I'm looking for a way to the release that I seek
To get rid of you must I get rid of me?
I'm scared that is how it will have to be

(19th August 2013)

4. Back from the Edge

Diary Entry 19th August 2013
I know he is here watching me. Nurse says I need to eat and sleep but I can't do it. The doctors have increased the haloperidol to make him go away but he won't shut up and the touching is awful. Plans are in place. P is coming tonight but I don't want him to bring C as he wouldn't understand why I can't let him touch me. It's not safe; I don't want him to contaminate anyone else.

Diary Entry 20th August 2013
So grim. Still no sleep and they say I haven't eaten for over a week. Saw the doctor and he is increasing the haloperidol again to see if it helps with the voice. He was worried about my weight and not eating but I told him that 'he' says if I eat then something bad will happen to P and the kids. I told the doctor I am contaminated and no one can touch me as it's too dangerous for them. He mentioned ECT if I don't eat and said they can do it without my permission as I am sectioned. I am distraught about this. They put me on a food and fluid chart and want me to have Fortisips [a nutritional protein drink] too, but how can I eat when something bad will happen? Everyone says it won't but I know he is absolutely real. The voice: shouting, laughing and touching is more real than they are to me. I don't feel real, like watching a person from far away. It looks like me, but I have no control over me. Don't know how else to explain it. If only they would give me the choice to decide if I stay or go and finish it off. If I die, he dies with me, and everyone is safe.

Diary Entry 22nd August 2013
Still here. Tried a Fortisip but he knows it is really food, and continues with his threat to hurt them, so I can't take the risk. The haloperidol makes me sleepy but it doesn't stop him. I know he is

real even though they try to talk me out of it. They keep saying I will be kept safe but I'm not if he's here, and nor are they. I'm still not real, I look funny in the mirror and not in control. P and the boys came but it's not safe for them. Doctor came and said they can't increase the meds until I eat because they are strong. She said if I haven't eaten when she is back after the weekend, I can be zapped without my consent. I do not want this but apparently my choice and wishes can be overridden.

Diary Entry 25th August 2013
P came to see me to try to get me to eat. Miss the kids, not seen them for a long time especially A and think she is mad at me. How will ECT even work? Surely the priority should be to get rid of the voice then maybe I can start eating when he's not threatening to hurt them? I just can't risk it, I can't. If they would just concentrate on getting rid of him, I wouldn't need ECT.

Diary Entry 31st August 2023
Should have written this before now but each day runs into a blur of horribleness. Had a session of ECT without my consent and it was truly awful. Have another planned for Monday and, once again, I won't be consenting. Surely this can't carry on. Why can't he just leave me alone? He took all he wanted from me then, what more is there to take? But it's not just me he wants, he wants them too. My plan needs to work.

Diary Entry 15th September 2013
It's Sunday and stupidly quiet – no-one around. I seem to have missed 2 weeks out. They found my hidden tablets, I was in trouble and I handed the tie in to the staff. Now I have nothing and no plans to do anything. Still having the ECT, have one tomorrow and the last one was with me consenting. Think my mood has been getting better. I miss everyone at home and should be there for A and B going back to uni. I am eating proper food now but my trousers are loose so

I must have lost weight. I need to keep on top of writing this because I can't remember what happens and I'm very confused. Not really sure how long I have been here.

I completed the course of ECT, my mental state continued to improve, and I stabilised and was discharged after three months, on lots of medication. My therapy was stopped for a while then reintroduced as a short course of compassionate mind therapy before recommencing the trauma-focused CBT.

I continued to work with G to process the trauma and settled into the twice-weekly sessions and day-to-day life with my family. As the work progressed, things became harder again and my PTSD became more unmanageable. In April 2014, I had input from the home treatment team for two weeks as thoughts of self-harm and suicide again became difficult. I knew I needed to continue the work with G but over the summer this became more and more difficult. I started to restrict food intake in an effort to feel in control, my mood deteriorated, I did not sleep, the nightmares and flashbacks increased in intensity, I had dissociative periods and the voice returned. My community psychiatric nurse arranged a mental health assessment, but I took an overdose of my medication, and was admitted to hospital on a section 2, which was then changed to another section 3.

I did not write a diary at this time as it did not feel safe to me to write things down and I have limited memories of this period.

In January 2015 I had a review and ECT was considered but I said no. According to my notes, my antipsychotic medication was changed, and the intensive trauma therapy continued on the ward. After six months, my family questioned whether I should have ECT again as it had worked on the previous occasions and the trauma therapy was not really progressing as I was so unwell. I had a locum consultant at this time and he was not keen for me to have ECT despite the wishes of my family and other professionals involved in my care. As my section was coming up for review, there was a tribunal meeting where everyone involved expressed their opinion.

Report from Psychologist G, 20th April 2015

As you are aware, I have been seeing K for a number of months. We are working on processing her trauma memories utilising trauma-focused CBT. K has engaged very well with the model, and generally works extremely hard both during our sessions and when completing homework tasks. Unfortunately, her mood seems to have dipped considerably, she has noticed that both the frequency and intensity of her auditory hallucinations have increased, to the point where I think she finds it extremely difficult to concentrate on anything else. Unfortunately, this is also impacting negatively on her mood; although it may well be that it is a function of her low mood or a symptom of her low mood. I saw her on the ward yesterday; she had not eaten for 4 days, is neglecting her self-care, which is extremely unlike her, and is not currently in a position to do any psychological work. She is extremely suicidal at present. In the past, when she has experienced periods of extremely low mood, a course of ECT has been the only thing that has lifted her mood and allowed her to engage fully in a therapeutic process, as well as to function on a day-to-day basis. I would therefore strongly advise a further course of ECT before K's mental state deteriorates further.

Report from Community Psychiatric Nurse 20th April 2015

K has been prescribed a multitude of different antidepressants and mood stabilisers in various combinations and, in more recent years, antipsychotic medication has been included into her treatment plan. K has responded well to a number of courses of ECT over the years. K does not prefer ECT but does recognise, at times of severe depression and when her risk to herself is high, then ECT is necessary. In the community, in addition to on-going CMHT [Community Mental Health Team] support, K has engaged with Rape Crisis for a long period of individual therapy, worked briefly with the community team psychologist and has been seeing G since 2012 for trauma-focused CBT. This has continued whilst K has remained an inpatient and most recently K and G have been meeting 3 times a week to work intensively through her narrative. K clearly states that, if her treatment plans ultimately fail to improve her mental health, she will end her life. K constantly struggles with the fear that her problems are too much of a burden to the family and, at times, feels just unable to continue with life with the extent and disabling effects of her symptoms.

P is very concerned about the current health of K, her diet and restriction of eating. K is currently not eating and only drinking minimally. P has long term serious concerns about K's safety. He has experienced numerous occasions where K has harmed herself and attempted to kill herself. In recent weeks, K's mental health has deteriorated and P feels that his concerns and requests have not been addressed by doctors. He feels that K currently has, for some weeks, needed ECT but feels his concerns have not been taken into account.

K has insight into her difficulties and currently feels the lowest in mood she has ever felt. She has previously declined ECT treatment even though she recognises it has improved her mood. In her own words 'I hate ECT but I know I need it now.' K reports feeling unable to function at even a basic level and is neglecting her self-care, hasn't eaten for over a week and has constant suicidal thoughts and urges which make her feel guilty. K indicates that she does have an undisclosed suicidal plan.

K remains severely depressed and is losing hope in her own chances of recovery. K recognises the need for continued hospitalisation and treatment and now feels that she needs ECT treatment to enable her mood to improve. G, K, P and I all feel that K's current request to have ECT treatment as soon as possible is explored and expedited.

Following the tribunal my section was extended for a further six months, the CBT temporarily suspended and I commenced another course of ECT with the aim of elevating my mood and improving symptoms to enable me to re-engage with the therapy. Once again, this worked, and the therapy started again on the ward, with a longer-term plan of maintenance ECT treatment alongside the therapy.

On the 9th September 2015, after a year detained in hospital, I was discharged home to continue the CBT and maintenance ECT treatment in the community. To this date, I have not required any further admissions to hospital. I continued with the maintenance ECT for around six months, with the time between treatments increasing from every two weeks to every four weeks until I made the decision to stop completely. I continued the trauma-focused CBT for another six months after that.

I no longer have input from mental health services and no longer take any psychiatric medications. I have my life back, a life I value, cherish and, most of all, enjoy. Importantly, my family now have a wife, a mother, a grandmother, a daughter and a sister – things that were lost to them for too many years.

Did ECT cure me of my depression? – NO

Did ECT take my trauma away? – again NO

BUT it was an integral part of my treatment alongside medication and therapy. It was the intervention that lifted my mood to allow me to be able to engage with the therapy I so desperately needed. It stopped me wanting to die when I was actively trying to do just that.

I don't take being well for granted; I became unwell despite good diet and exercise, mindfulness and talking therapies, being surrounded by people who cared for me and having a comfortable life. I found myself, as the novelist Styron says, in the grip of a depression of a magnitude and intensity 'out of control', desperately trying to end my life. I know my history puts me at risk of further episodes of depression and, if that happens, I would absolutely consider ECT as a treatment again.

It would be disingenuous of me to speak about my experience of ECT as a purely positive one: there are risks and side effects, as with any treatment. I do have some autobiographical memory loss, mainly connected to the period when I was unwell. Holidays, events, people's names are missing from my memory. I can see myself in photos or look at things I posted that come up on Facebook, but I cannot recall what happened or being there. Some memories I lost have returned as time has gone on, but others remain stubbornly elusive despite me being reminded about them by others. I have childhood memories and memories of my life before I became unwell, I can make and retain new memories, I have been able to learn new skills and I can still remember and refer to knowledge I gained when I trained and worked as a children's nurse. Initially, I found I had some issues with words: I would know the word I wanted to say but was unable to recall it. It sometimes happens now, but to a much lesser degree. I do make notes and write appointments down, but I have always done that. There is a chance I might forget them if they were not on my phone or calendar, but I don't think that is unique to me or others who have had ECT. My concentration and decision making were greatly impaired when I became depressed, before I had ECT; they are not an issue now. I dislike not being able to remember events like family holidays but I balance it, and am able to accept it, because I am still here with my family living my life and watching them live theirs, and for many years that did not look possible.

I choose to share my story not because I want more people to have ECT, or because my experience has more validity than others, but for balance. Putting my head above the parapet by speaking about my experiences of ECT has made me a target on numerous occasions. I have been accused, openly, of being used by psychiatry to promote their interests, and have been subject to abuse via private messages telling me I'm lying or complicit in murder and brain damage and it would have been better if I had killed myself to save others who might be influenced by my story. Fear, stigma and misrepresentation exist and will persist because of the polarisation of views around ECT. It is a treatment that is neither all good nor all bad and there are many patients and families stuck in the middle trying to decipher the noise.

5

Two Sides of the Storm – A Couple's Story
Sally and Paul's Story

2019

Paul

Throughout the final two years of my career in banking, I felt increasingly exhausted, burnt out and disconnected. I had a senior role which, for many years, involved long hours, frequent nights away and, often, periods of significant stress and pressure. I was incredibly hard working, diligent and probably cared too much – so both my personality and my singular focus on work undoubtedly compounded things.

My new boss was seeking a commitment from me for a further two years in the role but, following a weekend of reflection, I decided to bring my thirty-seven-year career to a premature close. So, I declined the request and was fortunate to be able to negotiate a very graceful early retirement.

Initially, I felt incredibly elated and enjoyed the warm congratulations and plaudits from colleagues. But, very quickly, I began to feel deflated. Within only a few weeks of making the decision to retire, I felt extremely sad, lonely, and isolated. Shortly thereafter, anxiety and depression started to creep in, with ever increasing force and intensity.

Around this time we also decided to move house which, in hindsight, was a huge mistake. I should have paused and allowed myself to come to terms with retirement after thirty-seven years, which alone was a significant milestone. Instead, we pressed on with quite a major move, to a house that, whilst in a lovely location, required an awful lot of work. And that added significantly to my building sense of anxiety.

Sally

I could tell Paul was beginning to feel increasingly anxious. As the time came to leave work, I think he began to realise he had no plans for the future, and no real sense of purpose. He was given 'gardening leave' before his retirement officially started and he'd go into the office, even though there was no need – he said it was the only place he felt 'safe'. After a while, I got so worried that I rang his boss, asking if they could create some kind of part-time role or consultancy for a few months so he could gradually ease into not working. Sadly, they couldn't help. In a company which was always talking about the importance of recognising the mental well-being of their staff, when it came to someone actually becoming mentally ill, they just didn't seem to understand.

Although Paul had previously had times when he felt low and a little frazzled, this felt like something different. In the space of a few weeks, what seemed to start as low-level anxiety became all consuming.

Paul

My slide continued to gather pace and I recognised I needed help. So, I went to see my GP who prescribed medication followed, shortly after, by some sessions with a psychologist. However, during weekly visits, my GP could see that my condition continued to decline rapidly, and he transferred my care to the community mental health team initially – and then the crisis team.

Around this time, I started to experience what I now know were psychotic and delusional thoughts. I started to believe that I was a tax fraud and had not completed my tax returns properly for years … with a court appearance and prison the most likely outcome. It was utterly terrifying as I truly believed that I was a criminal and had brought shame on my family. I remember one day when I saw a cyclist outside our gates taking photos of the house and I became convinced he was from the Inland Revenue, building a case against me. In reality, we live in an Art Deco property, which, apparently, is of interest to local art/architecture students.

Also, my feelings about the house started to completely overwhelm me as I worried about various repairs and improvements which were required, alongside things that could go wrong or might need fixing. I became fixated about the flat roof of the property requiring extensive repairs, and leaks ruining the property. I also became terrified that a large oak tree would blow over in the wind and cause terrible damage to our neighbour's property. The fact that I had just retired and didn't have a regular income weighed heavily, and I feared that I might have brought financial disaster upon the family.

Sally

From worries about the house collapsing to undeclared tax bills, my husband had become a tortured soul. His paranoia was growing daily, to the point where he had lost touch with reality. Small-scale worries had become impending catastrophic events.

Having had no experience of mental illness, I could only relate my husband's condition to that of my late mother's Alzheimer's – no matter how long and how hard you try and rationalise, he could not be convinced out of his worst fears. I remember trying to convince him that the roof was solid and not about to collapse. I had more than one builder round to inspect – but all to no avail. I employed a tax accountant to address his fears about not paying enough tax. Even if Paul had made a few mistakes with his tax (which he hadn't), the result would be a fine, not prison – but despite the accountant confirming this, he could not be convinced. Despite help and medication from the GP and community health crisis team, his condition got worse and worse – and quickly. I struggled to hold down my own job, shield our eleven-year-old son and, at the same time, make sure my husband wasn't left alone with his demons for too long.

'Please let me die' ... not the words you ever want to hear from the love of your life. But, with the morning sun streaming into our beautiful new house, these were the first words I would hear from Paul when he awoke. Thanks to some recently prescribed sleeping pills he had slept for a few hours, but now I woke up to his pained expression looking at me. Another day, another day of suffering – one for which the only way out seemed to be suicide.

Paul

After only a few weeks, I reached a tipping point and things started to spiral rapidly out of control. The pain I was experiencing was unrelenting and the only way out I could see was just not to be here anymore. Suicidal thoughts quickly developed and I entered what was later referred to as a 'rehearsal phase', planning different ways to end my life.

By this stage I could barely function. I'd sit in a chair in our lounge all day, unable to focus and with awful thoughts constantly circulating. It was an effort even to wash up. I'd go to bed around 7pm, mainly to try and avoid my eleven-year-old son seeing me in so much pain . . . and I'd lie there awake for hours, ruminating. I was exhausted. Zoplicone delivered temporary respite, providing a couple of hours sleep, but I'd wake up in the middle of the night in an anxious state and with a bitter, metallic taste in my mouth. Day after day this pattern repeated with no respite.

It was an incredibly frightening and traumatic period. I had this sensation of being trapped in sinking sand and the harder I fought for control, the more I was getting pulled under. Panic and fear were a constant feature and utterly exhausting – and the only way I could think of stopping the intense pain was to end my own life. And, at times, out of a perverse sense of love, care and worry for my family, I sometimes wondered whether an end might be the best outcome for all of us, which is such a distorted thought to have had, but perhaps illustrates how unwell I had become.

Sally

He begged me to let him go. I begged him, for the sake of his son, not to take his own life. I worried about leaving him on his own, so always had another adult in the house. I know he went for walks to a nearby gorge and thought about throwing himself off. I took his car keys away as I felt driving could be dangerous. It was desperate. Paul then started to talk about us all three 'going together'. I knew in my heart that Paul wouldn't hurt us, but I also knew that something had to be done before it was too late. I knew the crisis team had a duty of care, especially with a child involved, so I called them late on a Friday begging them to help. Finally, the team said they thought he should go to hospital – effectively, be sectioned.

Paul

One fateful day, early on a Saturday morning in July 2019, I climbed a nearby cliff wall. I don't think it was with the intention of jumping, but there was no doubt I was rehearsing. Having been persuaded by a passer-by to climb down, I mentioned the incident to my wife and I think it was this which started the process of sectioning. The next day, a team from the crisis department turned up . . . .

Sally

It was a weekend when the sectioning took place, and I made sure my son was out of the house with friends. It was one of the worse days of my life – Paul cried in fear and despair as four large men made sure he accompanied them into a blacked-out people carrier and drove him away. Before they took him away, he tried to run up to the attic and onto the roof of the house. Luckily, I had the key. He didn't resist going, but he was terrified. And it was terrifying. It was also surreal – how could this have got so bad so quickly? A few months earlier he was a 'normal' middle-aged guy, looking forward to taking his foot off the pedal and leaving a job which had become very stressful. We had a great life, with the house of our dreams and a lovely young son, and with all three of us fit and healthy. Now, he was being carted off in a blacked-out vehicle to be locked away in a secure psychiatric ward in another town about an hour away (as there were no beds nearby).

The day of the sectioning, though, was also a huge relief to me, as I knew that, for the time being, he was safe and I could take a rest from the constant watch I felt I had to keep on him. But it was also only the start of another long and difficult journey.

Paul

And so began a journey of 109 days in two different mental health hospitals. I found the hospital environment really chaotic and the whole experience pretty terrifying. Being in a ward with twenty other disturbed individuals wasn't an experience which I found to be conducive to recovery. I was given ever increasing doses of multiple different types of drugs, but I got no better at any stage. The psychotic thoughts continued and this time I feared that my property would be robbed whilst I was in hospital and my family held hostage and to ransom. At one stage, I cut up all my bank cards to avoid being robbed by fellow patients ... or even, as my imagination had me believe, the staff!

Sally

As the weeks went by, he didn't seem to be improving – at all. If anything, his fears, although different, were just as intense (now more about being beaten up or murdered in hospital or being made to rob his own house). He was also losing lots of weight, and was unable to walk more than a few steps, being convinced he would collapse from the strain.

I visited every other day, hoping to see improvement – but there was none. Every day Paul would text me – always messages full of fear and paranoia ... hundreds of texts. For example:

Today is definitely the day that everything gets compromised. People have been asking for lots of details. Address and finances will be revealed ... then I will be kicked out. This is devastating for all of us.

Don't come – I just don't think it's safe for you here anymore and I will barely be able to stand tomorrow. There are more dangerous patients who have arrived opposite me today ... definitely not safe for you.

I've been drugged up to the eyeballs by staff and will pass out in the next hour. Absolutely convinced it's part of their plan to rob us and there's nothing we can do to stop them.

Different drugs were tried, including various antidepressants and antipsychotic drugs. And gradually the doses increased as the weeks went on – but with no change at all. Then ECT was talked about for the first time.

Paul

After more than three months with no improvement in my condition whatsoever, the psychiatrist asked me to consider ECT. However, based on the little I knew, I was incredibly reluctant. I am of the of the generation that remembers the film *One Flew Over the Cuckoo's Nest* – that was the extent of my knowledge of ECT, and I certainly wasn't going to allow that to happen to me!

I was handed some basic information to read and given a brief tour of the theatre where ECT was administered, but I didn't find that reassuring at all.

As a consequence of my reluctance, the hospital team was at the point of giving up and discharging me, much to the exasperation of my wife, because she knew that I was no better and that we would go right back round the circle again. She did a lot of research, which she discussed with me, and she persuaded me to give ECT a go. She was the one person I trusted, and she was fighting for me every step of the way. And so, despite being terrified the doctors were trying to punish me, I agreed to give it a go for her sake, and for my son.

Sally

I'd heard vaguely of ECT but assumed it was a thing of the past – and a barbaric one at that. Then I started reading about it and talking to people. It seemed that the success rate for people with severe depression was surprisingly high. But I also read about patients who were very anti-ECT and those who claimed they had suffered terrible memory loss. However, medical professionals, including our own GP (who I trusted completely), were highly positive about it. It seemed worth a go – and anyway, we had run out of alternatives.

Paul took some persuading – but I think he too could see it might be his only way out of what had become a living hell. He was given two sessions a week. After a couple of sessions, he seemed to get quite angry, more frustrated – but the psychiatrist (who took the brunt of his verbal anger) thought it was a good sign – that he was gaining more energy.

Paul

Ahead of the first session, I remember being incredibly scared and I contemplated sabotaging the treatment by drinking water, which was something we were required not to do. However, the first session was scheduled and I remember being walked across the garden to a separate ward for the treatment. It was a pretty terrifying walk, contemplating the unknown and fearing what was about to happen. Once I was in the theatre, a kindly anaesthetist and other staff offered some reassurance, and I was quickly given a sedative. The next thing I knew I was waking up in a recovery room, being offered some tea and a piece of toast, and then returning to the ward.

I think any initial fear and trauma I had was, largely, removed following the first treatment. And in any case, my state of mind was such that I'd pretty much given up at this stage anyway. In terms of offering reassurance to anyone contemplating ECT, I'd say that there's nothing really to fear from the procedure itself, which doesn't take too long to administer. You're given a general anaesthetic so are not awake during the procedure – and I understand that a muscle relaxant is always administered.

Treatments two and three followed quite rapidly, and I remember the psychiatrist saying to my wife that he then noticed I had an awful lot more fight about me. I was getting angry and I walked out of one of his ward rounds, objecting to what I felt were his patronising questions. The psychiatrist saw that as a good sign – that I had some energy and some fight back again!

Sally

After five sessions I had a phone call from one of the nurses: 'I think you ought to come to the hospital now', she said in a bright and breezy manner. Apparently Paul had gone to the front desk to enquire as to when he could see his beloved son – something he hadn't felt able to do for months.

As soon as I arrived and looked at his face, I could tell – it was a complete turnaround. The old Paul I knew was back. I can only describe the sudden and dramatic change in him as a complete miracle.

He couldn't immediately remember all his treatment (although these memories did come back), but he knew he had gone through a fundamental change. It was as if his brain had been 're-booted'. The paranoia, the desperate fears, the crippling anxiety and all the physical symptoms associated with the illness were gone – just like that.

Paul

After session number five something quite profound happened. Rather than deep, dark thoughts of doom and despair, I was talking with positivity about the future, about wanting to see my son. My wife visited and we saw the psychiatrist shortly after – and he actually jokingly said that I would only have one more session of the original twelve because he didn't want to 'make me too happy'!

Sally

Was it real? Would it last? I couldn't quite believe it. Paul had a final session of ECT and he was declared fit enough to be discharged. The first time he was allowed out of the hospital on his own (as the fear of him hurting himself had resided), he called me on the mobile. Elated, he described the joy of the sun on his face as he walked across a car park to a local superstore – not the surroundings you'd expect to call heaven! But for him it was – he was free, his demons dispelled, another chance to live again. I cried with joy and relief at his new-found freedom and happiness.

Paul

I remember being granted unaccompanied leave and walking across to the local superstore with the sun shining on my face. It felt entirely magical! Shortly after I was allowed home for a day and night, which went incredibly well. It was wonderful to sleep in a comfortable bed, in a quiet and familiar environment and to spend an hour soaking in a hot bath – pure joy! The simple things in life! I was discharged fully within a matter of days following session six, and am delighted to say that, nearly five years on, I have remained well ever since.

Looking back, the whole experience feels quite surreal . . . but, at the same time, I know only too well that the experience is incredibly real and not one I would ever wish to repeat. However, it has given me a real, deep understanding of mental ill health and just how powerful the mind can be. There's so much more that we need to do to develop a deeper and more sophisticated understanding of mental health – and to invest in much better and more effective treatments. Humans seem to have made huge advances in the treatment of many physical health conditions in recent times. Sadly, the same doesn't appear to apply to mental health. And with demand seemingly increasing year on year, there appears to be an increasingly urgent need to improve treatments and care.

Sally

ECT doesn't work for everyone, but for us (and many others) it is a miracle. It's a strong word, 'cure', but in Paul's case, and, looking back now nearly five years with no relapse, I can honestly say I believe ECT was a 'cure' – a lifesaving one.

6

The Long Way Home
Lucy's Story

I am thirty-six years old, married and live independently with my husband, Dave. I work in Service User Involvement for an NHS trust in England. I'm a member of the Service User Council and I sit on a number of steering groups. But life has not always been so kind to me ...

At the age of twenty-five, I was placed in a secure mental health unit. I would then spend the next eight years of my life in various psychiatric units.

What led to this is a bit of a blur in my memory, but I will try to relate the events as well as I can. I grew up in Hertfordshire with my loving parents and younger brother. I had a very good childhood, with many happy family holidays. I took part in the local Girl Guides group, danced ballet and played the flute. I enjoyed school and was focused on getting good results so I could go to university to study speech and language therapy. However, at school I felt a lot of pressure and became very stressed during my A levels. My uncle also passed away, which I found very difficult as we were very close. I was referred to the school counsellor, who was based in the school library. All my peers knew where I was going as I was passing through the library, which made me feel self-conscious. This was the beginning of my struggles with mental health.

I got the grades required to go to university and was fortunate to receive a grant, which my care coordinator organised, to get me access to a laptop and money to purchase textbooks for the course. I was given extra support by a mentor and I had 25 per cent extra time in exams. Money was also set aside for Pilates classes and regular massages, which helped me with stress levels. I completed the course and was awarded a distinction in speech, language and communication studies.

However, by then my mental health was in real decline and, from the age of twenty-three, I became an inpatient in local mental health units, followed by an out-of-area personality disorder unit

6. The Long Way Home

and, eventually, a low secure ward. Over time, I was diagnosed with schizophrenia, bipolar disorder and schizoaffective disorder. I started to believe that I could fly, so I would climb on the top of the sofa and jump from there, smashing my head on many occasions. I visited medical hospitals a number of times and I remember one time when I had huge black eyes where I had bashed my head on the floor. This belief lasted for five years or so.

I was always on at least one-to-one observation: there was one nurse with me all the time, day and night. Occasionally, there were two nurses allocated to look after me: two-to-one observation. Being in a secure environment was extremely difficult; to get out of the building you had to pass through at least two locked doors, toiletries were kept in locked cupboards and the TV and remote control were behind a secure cabinet. The unit had strict regimes for medication, eating and activity times, with very little time to go outside for fresh air. Visits from family and friends were restricted and supervised by a member of staff. I particularly remember my bedroom in this unit. It was small: there was just a bed, with a single cabinet for clothes, a built-in wardrobe and a sink, and that is all it had. It was at the end of the corridor, and it had no curtains on the window. Through the window I could see the secure garden surrounded by a fence that was as tall as the building. They must have regarded me as a risk for a long time, as I spent six years on this unit.

One day, I remember taking the mop from a cleaner and trying to attack her with it. I thought that I could fly away on the mop. The cleaner tried to get it back from me and I started fighting with her. Some of her colleagues and other staff members came to help her, so I threatened to hit her with the mop. I felt like I had some power in an environment where I had none. At that point, I was given a diagnosis of paranoid schizophrenia. I was also assessed for a diagnosis of autism when sent to a newly established personality disorder unit 50 miles from home. I had been at the unit no more than three weeks when the consultant psychiatrist said she believed that I did not have a personality disorder and that I might have bipolar disorder. Following an assessment, I was told I didn't have bipolar, but I could possibly have autism.

The psychiatrist who did the autism assessment concluded that I met thirteen of the eighteen categories to be diagnosed as autistic. My parents were present at the assessment and were asked many questions too. They asked this psychiatrist if he could recommend a programme to help with the autism. He told them that it would be the responsibility of the unit I was a patient in, but the staff had little, or no, knowledge of autism. Despite my diagnosis, I was sent to a low secure unit, 35 miles from home and was there for nearly three years. At this unit I received various treatments, including the medication clozapine.

After two years, I stopped taking the clozapine due to an upsetting incident in my life. I was given an injection of haloperidol and placed in seclusion. Unfortunately, I had an allergic reaction to the haloperidol and ended up in intensive care for a month, with neuroleptic malignant syndrome. I later found out that this is a very rare but dangerous side effect of antipsychotic drugs, which can present with high temperature, changes in blood pressure, muscle stiffness and other problems. I must have had a really bad form of this side effect, as I was in a coma for most of that month and was having seizures. I ended up having blood transfusions and dialysis. Then things got even worse. When I woke up from the coma, I became very paranoid. I was so paranoid I thought I was being poisoned, although I didn't think of any specific reasons for that, and I didn't trust anybody. I stopped eating to avoid being poisoned with the food. I went from being around 17 stone to almost 5 stone. After about a year, I had completely stopped eating and was being fed through a nasogastric (NG) tube to keep me alive. Due to the rapid weight loss, I was in and out of physical health hospitals and would often pull the NG tube out as I no longer wanted to live.

6. The Long Way Home

It was decided by my psychiatrist that I should have a course of ECT at the local general hospital. My parents were very reluctant, so my psychiatrist took them and my social worker to see the ECT clinic and to meet the team providing the treatment. They were given information on how it was going to be administered and felt reassured by what they were told. The ECT clinic was held in the hospital's eye-clinic, which was adapted twice a week to carry out the ECT procedure. I didn't want to have ECT, and I was taken to the clinic against my will and under restraint. The treatment happened early in the morning, and staff would get me out of bed and take me to the hospital in a van that was waiting outside the hospital reception. The journey took 30 minutes and four or five staff had to travel with me and hold me as I was fighting with them and shouting, despite being very thin and having an extremely frail body.

I was taken through the hospital in a wheelchair, trying to fight with the staff and shouting as I travelled through the corridors. To make things worse, I was so thin and dehydrated that the anaesthetist couldn't find a vein to insert a needle to give me medication. They had to insert a PICC line (Peripherally Inserted Central Catheter) and hold me down for the anaesthetic until I fell asleep. It was upsetting, being held down, but the psychiatrist and the team thought that I would die if I did not have the treatment. My parents and wider staff agreed, and the treatment took place.

After eight sessions, I still did not eat anything and I asked for the treatment to be stopped. It was decided by the medical team that ECT had not worked: a break in treatment was accepted and I was encouraged to engage in psychology. I was moved to the hospital rehabilitation ward where my mental health declined, including food refusal. ECT was prescribed again, and I went reluctantly. This time I had the full twelve treatments which resulted in me eating again and my mood lifted. After each session, I would go to the hospital café and get a milkshake. This was a real treat, and I would go less reluctantly to treatment. At the rehabilitation unit, I remember having my own room, I had access to a garden, I felt freer and could watch what I wanted on TV. We could cook and do our own activities. Perhaps it was this change in environment that helped me get better, alongside the ECT. I think there was a shift in my mental state, I wanted the treatment to work and to get better. During this time my parents visited twice a week, on a Wednesday afternoon and at the weekend. Extended family members and friends also visited. I began vocational work in the hospital grounds, including feeding the fish and other animals. I took part in a lot of art activity and sold some, with the proceeds going to the local general hospital and mental health charities, raising over £2,000.

After, I was moved to another rehabilitation unit, this time near Brighton, more than two hours from home. I was eating and drinking, initially, but was really badly bullied by some of the other women on the ward, so I stopped eating again. The doctor wanted to prescribe ECT again; however, the local NHS didn't want to because, they said, I was an out-of-county patient and they would have had to negotiate funding for the treatment to be carried out in another hospital. I actually agreed to have ECT, but they continued to deny it to me. I thought this was awful: that I was being denied treatment that I knew would help. I spent a while in the local intensive care unit as I was not eating or drinking. After a month in a general hospital, I started to engage in weekly psychology sessions.

I was feeling better, going to the gym, and eventually improved so much that they discharged me to supportive living in Hertfordshire near my family. By that time I was already thirty-three years old. I started doing service user involvement work as an Expert by Experience for the local NHS trust. I attended several meetings for the Trust, including interview panels for new staff, and I helped the local university recruit psychology

6. The Long Way Home

students. At the supported living I was initially seen by the Enhanced Rehabilitation Outreach Service (EROS): a team providing support for people who have been discharged from hospital. They are made up of nurses, social workers and support workers. The team were very proactive, and I would see them regularly: two or three times a week. The social worker helped me apply for benefits, and one of my goals was to make an omelette during cooking sessions.

They suggested that I do some work for the local mental health trust, and I obtained a grant for a gym membership. I enjoyed the gym and used to go swimming most days. I think that this regular exercise and the routine of going to the swimming pool helped me a lot with my recovery. I was also taking medication, and had psychotherapy and art therapy at the local mental health centre.

After being in supported living for two years, I married my husband. We met at school; Dave has given me so much support and we enjoy going on holiday regularly and eating out at local restaurants. He ensures that I take my medication and maintain a regular routine. I became settled doing service user involvement work and had nine hours support a week from a support worker.

Once I was an outpatient and living in my own home, I became unwell due to a blip in taking my medication and it was decided, by the psychiatric crisis team, that I should have a course of ECT in the community to help the recurring depression. I had my first treatment at the mental health ECT suite; however, due to my blood pressure measuring so high before receiving ECT, the treatment was moved to the local general hospital in the day surgery unit. After the treatment my oxygen levels became low, so the anaesthetist had to monitor this. Initially, I had twelve treatments: two a week, with the electric charge increasing. The team realised that my illness seems to be quite cyclical; I will be okay for a while but then will become unwell again. After the twelve sessions an agreement was made between the psychiatrist, the nursing team and me to continue with ECT maintenance therapy once a week, to see if that could stop that cyclical pattern. When unwell, I get very depressed, I don't go out and I become paranoid, believing that something bad will happen to my family or something will happen to me.

The treatment is a big commitment; first thing in the morning a taxi picks me up and takes me to the general hospital. After the treatment someone has to be with me for twenty-four hours to monitor for any adverse effects. This monitoring is done in shifts: my dad picks me up and drives me home, then my mum takes over. At 3pm my support worker comes, and then hands over to my husband in the evening. My family have noticed the deterioration in my memory but, on the whole, my mood has become a lot better.

Previously, when I was staying in hospital, I was on one-to-one observation, so would return to my room and sleep. However, now I am in the community it is expected that my family supervise me. I am also trying to continue with my Expert by Experience work, in an effort to be living a 'normal' life; at times I find this quite difficult. My memory is poor, and my sleep has been affected but, overall, I am grateful for the treatment. Something I have been thinking about, and talking to my parents about, now that I am still in treatment, is that I want to know more about the treatment, about the electric current, the voltage, the side effects. My parents will benefit too if they can have such a conversation, because my memory has deteriorated, and I have nobody to talk to about this. In the day surgery unit of the general hospital, I am the only patient having ECT, which can feel quite lonely.

Writing my story, and sharing it with others, has made me more confident and I feel able to come to terms with what I have experienced over almost two decades. It has helped me process what has happened to me. I am no longer jumping off furniture, but I feel as though I am now flying with success.

6. The Long Way Home

Added by George Kirov, September 2024: It wasn't very obvious whether Lucy was really benefitting from maintenance ECT until these developments during the late stages of the book's production. She had developed breathing problems after a seizure, requiring extra anaesthetics support. The team felt it was too dangerous to continue with ECT. The treatment was stopped and she was referred to have transcranial magnetic stimulation (TMS). I received further emails from Lucy a few months later, just before submitting the stories:

> How's the book going? Unfortunately I am in hospital. They are giving me TMS as there is a waiting list for ECT . . . I think stopping the ECT definitely affected my mood and my decisions. I stopped taking my antipsychotics . . . they were making me gain so much weight. I became psychotic and very depressed, and have constant suicidal thoughts. I was brought in by the police under a section 136 and then put on a section 2. I have lost weight so the anaesthetists are happy to go ahead with ECT as long as in a general hospital rather than the local psychiatric hospital.

7

Surviving Bipolar – ECT and the 'Self-Binding Directive'
Tania's Story

7. Surviving Bipolar: ECT and the 'Self-Binding Directive'

The Pregnancy

November 2015

It's November 2015. I'm seven months pregnant and lying on a bed in one of the main operating theatres at Northwick Park Hospital, wired up to multiple monitors and about to receive ECT. It's been relatively calm up to now. Everyone else has been frantically busy: transferring the ECT equipment to the main operating theatre from the mental health unit; liaising with the obstetrics team to get them up to speed; establishing who needs to be there and setting up the foetal monitoring. Now, though, things are ready. Very shortly, they'll be inserting the anaesthetic needle and I can feel the panic starting to set in. Outwardly, I'm calm. Inwardly, the terror starts to mount. Kathy, the lead ECT nurse, takes my hand, as I feel one solitary tear roll down my cheek. If they've spotted my reaction, I'm sure that the others will interpret this sudden shift of mood as concerns about the pregnancy. They've explained that foetal monitoring is in place throughout and a full obstetrics team present, just to cover the extremely unlikely risk that they might need to deliver the baby by caesarean while I'm unconscious. But Kathy knows that's not the reason – she squeezes my hand and whispers 'It'll be OK; you're doing the right thing. I know it's not easy, but this is the right thing to do.'

Things were pretty calm a few minutes beforehand. I chatted to a couple of nursing students as everything was being prepared. Wearing my 'researcher' and 'ECT advocate' hats, I talked about the effectiveness and safety of ECT as a medical procedure and voiced my concerns about the profound levels of stigma and misinformation surrounding this 'lifesaving' treatment. Once the clinical team was ready, everything suddenly felt very different.

Underneath my calm and composed exterior, my inner self is terrified. The voices which I have been hearing, and the 'presence'

I have felt growing over the last couple of weeks, are adamant that I must not proceed with ECT. Most of the time now, they appear far more real to me than the 'reality' of the world and people around me. The voices would be angry – this much I knew. As they had grown stronger during the past few days, they had remonstrated with me: 'Don't play along; don't tell them anything; don't sign the consent form.' But it is not simply the fear of their anger holding me back – it is the fear which comes from believing that they are right. Even while I am fully able to exist and communicate within a world of people I know and trust, people who are telling me that I am seriously unwell and that I need to be treated, this world seems false, and their assurances increasingly seem to stem from some type of complex malevolence.

With the clinical team prepared, I am suddenly the 'patient' once again: my speeding mind is caught in a tortuous cycle of deliberation as it races through the possible options for how to avoid treatment, and counters each possibility as fast as they came. As the needle goes in, I know the voices will be there. They will not allow me to have a moment of calm and enjoy the slide into oblivion as the anaesthetic takes hold. Instead, they will torment me, rebuking me for my weakness and capitulation.

This time, though, it feels very different. As the anaesthetic starts to course through my system, the rest of the room begins to fade and my mind is suffused with ethereal beauty. The Sirens are singing to me. The brief seconds before I lose consciousness expand into a moment of beauty and revelation as I realise that I, myself, am Odysseus, the only human to experience the song of the Sirens and stay alive, protected by the bindings. I know, also, that this is transient. Once gone, the moment can never be recaptured. The voices are showing me what I stand to lose if I continue with the treatment. Internally, as my consciousness slips away, I tell them I will be stronger, that I will find a way to get away and come to them. I cling to the music and beg them to hold me in that moment.

7. Surviving Bipolar: ECT and the 'Self-Binding Directive'

Bound to the Mast

Until the needle went in, I could have still called a stop to the procedure. Until the point at which I lost consciousness, the possibility remained open. But I also knew, only too well, that this would only serve to delay, rather than prevent, the ECT. Before the pregnancy, I had, essentially, committed myself to receive ECT if I became unwell during pregnancy. I knew that the chances of severe illness in the perinatal period were extremely high, that this would put my life at risk, and that illness would make me resistant to accepting the only treatment which I knew could work. I knew that providing a pathway towards the possibility of involuntary treatment via detention under the Mental Health Act or 'sectioning' would be the only way to ensure safety. I had created a 'self-binding' advance directive or 'Ulysses contract', in which I explained this to a clinical team and had, effectively, given a request and consent for this treatment to be given, despite the reluctance I knew I would feel.

In Greek mythology Odysseus, or Ulysses by his Roman name, asks his crew to bind him to the mast of the ship, and block their own ears with wax, so that he can hear the magical song of the Sirens but be safe from being lured to his death by their irresistible melody. He knew that his crew would not release him, no matter how hard he tried, while he experienced the enchantment of the Sirens' song and was powerless to resist the urge to join them, with the lethal consequences this action would hold. I had written my first self-binding directive, almost by chance, about eight years earlier. A few years after that, through a strange set of circumstances, my area of work had changed to medical ethics and law, and I had found myself working on the development of mental health advance directives in a professional context. My current illness was suddenly, and strangely, bringing together the personal and professional dimensions of my life, even merging within my own delusory reality. As often happens in mania and psychosis, the beliefs appeared to draw on elements of my inner life: making me believe myself to be Odysseus, experiencing the Sirens' song and, through some strange irony, almost literally being 'bound to the mast'.

Lying in the operating theatre, I find myself trapped, bound in by my own words, 'hoist with my own petard'. My own knowledge and understanding, when well, of the internal workings of my mind when severely unwell, combined with my increasing professional expertise in mental health ethics and law, mean that I've created a pretty watertight self-binding directive or 'Ulysses contract', and the chances of me managing to convince the clinical team that I no longer need ECT are almost non-existent. I know, only too well, that if I opt out of today's treatment, I'll face the same situation in a few days' time. My lack of cooperation will be interpreted as a sign of diminishing capacity and increasing risk, and the procedure will go ahead, most likely under the auspices of Section 62 of the Mental Health Act, which allows urgent treatment. No matter how articulately I would be able to present my concerns, I am bound by my own prior words and, for now, trying to remain outwardly calm and accept that the inevitability of treatment is the only feasible option.

An Explanation: The Fusion of My Personal and Professional Lives

So, what was I doing having ECT during my pregnancy? Why on earth, in the twenty-first century, would anyone, let alone a heavily pregnant women, resort to ECT? And that's where my work and my personal life overlap. As I'll explain, my first treatment with ECT long predated my work in this area, as did my first advance choice document. At the time, each of these represented something of a 'last chance' in terms of making an impact on my illness and protecting me from the self-destruction towards which it was impelling me. My illness, which I now know to be a severe, mixed affective form of bipolar I disorder, makes me acutely unwell and, as it oscillates between manic energy, euphoria and disinhibition, terrifying psychotic visions, voices and messages, and a feverish and intolerable internal detachment and agitation, the one consistent feature is the uncontrollable drive towards self-destruction.

Having been severely unwell in the years following the birth of my older daughter, I knew that trying for a second child would present an enormous risk, especially since, with the exception of ECT and maintenance ECT, we had not discovered any successful medical maintenance strategy to keep things stable and prevent relapse. Having been relatively stable for a few years at the end of my thirties, my husband and I began to wonder if there might be any possibility of trying for a second child, an option which we'd previously abandoned due to the risk of illness and risk to my life. Following a consultation with a perinatal specialist, we were confronted very directly with the risks that another pregnancy might hold. The psychiatrist told me, with a combination of directness and compassion, that, judging by my medical history of the past few years, and the link between my condition and hormonal factors, the chances that I would become severely mentally unwell either during a future pregnancy or in the postnatal period, or both, was more than 50 per cent. Seeing the crestfallen look on our faces as we heard the statistics, he then went on to add:

> Having said that, looking at your medical history over the past few years, the chances that you'll become severely unwell during the next few years anyway are also at least 50 per cent and probably more. So, in some ways, you might as well go for it, put plans in place to keep yourself safe, and hopefully you'll at least end up with another child, if that's what you both want.

Following the consultation, we did a lot of research. By that time, I had started to work in the area of mental health, with a focus mainly on ethics and law. I had a strong interest in neuropsychiatry, stimulated largely by my experiences of ECT. I knew that I had to have a treatment plan in case I got pregnant and became unwell. I also knew that, realistically, having failed to respond to any type of mood stabilising or antidepressant medication, the only feasible option was ECT. I had heard, anecdotally, that ECT was safe in pregnancy, and I soon set about digesting all the research literature I could find. As you can imagine, studies on ECT in pregnancy are few and far between, owing to the rarity of the treatment and the impossibility of conducting any type of major clinical trial. However, there was a small but convincing set of observational studies, case studies and other anecdotal evidence which pointed quite clearly to ECT being a comparatively safe treatment to have during pregnancy in terms of effects on both mother and foetus.

By then, I knew much more about creating well-put-together advance choice documents. With the help of the clinical team, I set about creating a combination of a birth/pregnancy plan and a 'self-binding' advance choice document, which indicated very clearly the importance of liaison between maternity and psychiatry. Most importantly, I stated very clearly that research shows that ECT is safe and effective in pregnancy and that, given the risk to my life and my treatment resistance to other options, should I become severely unwell during pregnancy, I would like to be given ECT, even if I was objecting to it at the time.

Until the third trimester, the pregnancy was going extremely well. Physically, I was doing well, finding pregnancy easy and managing to continue with my running and other training. I looked and felt like a happy and healthy expectant mother. Shortly after entering the final trimester, my appearance and physical health remained the same. However, internally, my mind rapidly fell to pieces. As it always had been, the descent into a severe mixed state was almost instantaneous and clearly recognisable. We made arrangements to see the consultant psychiatrist and the wheels kicked into motion. Within 48 hours, psychosis and mania had well and truly set in, with my mind pushing me not to listen to the people around me and trying to convince me that I needed to resist any form of treatment and get as far away as possible as soon as I could. Fortunately for me, these patterns of illness were so well known to my family and the clinical team that I was left with no chance to escape or to evade treatment. That's how I found myself lying in the operating theatre, listening to the Sirens' song and waiting for ECT.

A few months later, I'm sitting at home, cradling my newborn daughter. The psychosis has lifted and, although fragile, I'm much better than I was. There's a ring at the door and it's Kathy from the ECT team. She's come round to see me and to meet my baby daughter. She hands me a gift – some lovely baby clothes – and we hug before I pass my daughter to her for a cuddle. We've become closer than ever through the last period of treatment – more like old close friends than patient and nurse. Kathy smiles down at the baby and we both relax.

A Year and a Half Later

It's a bright May morning, as I make my way to the Royal College of Psychiatrists, clutching my backpack and rehearsing my presentation. On the train, I reviewed my lecture notes and slides, checking that everything was in order and would make sense, going through my usual pre-conference checks. Today, though, is a very different presentation from anything I've done before. I'm presenting to the ECTAS (ECT Accreditation Service) annual conference. Later that morning I'll go up on the stage, alongside the ECT team from Northwick Park, and talk the audience through the logistics, processes and, now, the experience of ECT during pregnancy. The talk goes very well.

Despite the evidence pointing to its safety and effectiveness, ECT is very rarely given during pregnancy, and the audience seems fascinated to hear more about how this process was carried out at Northwick Park. The anaesthetist, consultant and nurses talk everyone through their roles and then it's my turn. I stand before the lectern, explaining about the circumstances. I talk briefly through how we reviewed the evidence prior to the pregnancy, and how we were satisfied that it would be safe were I to become unwell during pregnancy. I then describe my symptoms at the time of the treatment, how many treatments were given and the course of remission. My last slide shows a picture of my baby daughter, taken on her first birthday. With a beaming smile she sits in a makeshift ball-pit – a small paddling pool filled with brightly coloured balls. 'Without the possibility of ECT', I explain, 'I could never have risked embarking on this pregnancy. Without receiving ECT, I would never have survived it.'

My Own Experiences of ECT

Where It Started

I first had ECT when I was twenty-one. I had dropped out of my second year at university after becoming severely ill. Diagnosed with 'atypical depression', I became progressively more unwell as multiple different antidepressants failed to restore reality, destroy detachment and prevent the rapid deterioration of my speeding mind. Finally, it reached the point – now all too familiar – where my malfunctioning brain presented a serious risk to my life. I was referred for my first ever psychiatrist's appointment, at the Bristol Royal Infirmary. My dad came to Bristol to accompany me to the appointment. It was there I learnt, after I replied 'no' to the psychiatrist's questions about any family history of mental illness, that my maternal grandma

7. Surviving Bipolar: ECT and the 'Self-Binding Directive'

had experienced two 'breakdowns', for which she'd been hospitalised. It was also there, as I answered the clinical assessment questions, that I was told, for the first time, that, given how unwell I was and the level of risk, it would be necessary for me to be admitted to hospital.

A few months later, after multiple admissions and one failed suicide attempt, following an escape from 'close observation' in hospital, whilst at the funeral of one of their oldest friends my parents started talking to someone who turned out to be a consultant psychiatrist. When they told him about my predicament, and the fact that my condition was failing to respond to any type of treatment, he immediately asked about ECT. My oldest brother was a psychiatrist and, although by that time he was working in pharmaceuticals and no longer practised, he was very familiar with ECT and had seen it have remarkable results amongst his most severely unwell patients. By that point, I was so detached from everything around me that I agreed to give it a try. I had never heard of ECT, but was reassured about its safety and effectiveness by my brother.

I had eight treatments in total. After the sixth treatment, I woke up and knew immediately that something was very different. All at once, I could see that the perceived glass screen which had separated me from the people and world around me was no longer there. It took many months to make a full recovery. The months of illness, detachment and hospitalisation had left me with residual feelings of depression and social anxiety. But, restored to the 'real' world once again, I was able to engage with cognitive behaviour therapy (CBT) and gradually rebuild.

What was also highly evident, and has remained true throughout subsequent episodes in later years, is that there was no correlation between the mental disturbance and drive towards self-destruction and my well self or my external circumstances. Before becoming unwell, I had a fantastic first year at Bristol

University. For me, becoming an undergraduate felt, intellectually, like 'coming home'. For the first time, I was able to engage with my studies with what felt like an adequate level of depth and complexity, free from the constraints of an A-level syllabus and examinations. I loved both Bristol and my course and flourished both in and outside of my studies. When I was not studying, I had lots of friends, a new boyfriend (who would later become my husband) and a passion for music. I was always busy – socialising, studying or playing in orchestras and ensembles.

What I only realised, many years later, after finally being diagnosed with bipolar, was that my first year at university, which I think of as one of the best years of my life and which set the path for so much of my future, was also an extended period of being mildly 'high' or in a state of 'high-functioning hypomania'. In themselves, my actions were not problematic or clearly indicative of illness. But I now recognise that a year of intense activity, heightened energy and minimal sleep was also laying the groundwork for my first severe episode of illness. Eventually, there was a catalyst or 'trigger'. On coming back from holiday at the end of the summer, I was told that a close friend had been killed in an accident. Very abruptly, my 'high' was over. As the shock coursed through my system, I felt as if a wall or glass screen had descended between myself and the people and the world around me.

There were no lasting cognitive effects from the illness or the ECT. Later that year, I returned to university for the third and final year of my undergraduate degree and achieved a first in my final exams. Now that I was better, my heart was firmly set on academia. I received a scholarship from the British Academy, achieved a distinction in my MA at University College London and, sponsored by King's College London, embarked on my PhD in ancient philosophy. I was incredibly lucky to work with two inspirational supervisors and to have fantastic opportunities for lecturing undergraduates in London and Cambridge.

7. Surviving Bipolar: ECT and the 'Self-Binding Directive'

ECT in My Thirties and Forties

Shortly after starting my PhD, I got married. I remained well and stable for many years, without any type of maintenance treatment or psychological therapy. The memory of my illness stayed with me, but, as time went on, it became increasingly remote. I thought little about it and, although part of me was aware that it could recur, a deep and sometimes unrealistic optimism within me began to believe that it had been an isolated occurrence. I was aware that, should I decide to start a family, pregnancy and the perinatal period would present a risk to someone with my history. At this point, however, I had no real knowledge of how that might manifest or how to manage the associated risks.

I was lucky to fall pregnant for the first time when I was thirty. My daughter was born, and amidst the happiness, my family watched carefully in case there were any signs of depression, which was still, at that point, the diagnosis for my earlier episode. After my first child was born, I once again entered a long period of heightened energy and happiness. I, and other people, had no concerns about my health, as I looked after my daughter, lectured part time, qualified and worked as a personal trainer, and competed in a triathlon and a marathon. Looking back, it's now obvious to us all that I was, once again in a high-functioning extended state of hypomania. But the only thing that people were worried about was the darkness and self-destructiveness. Nobody thinks it's abnormal if you're not getting much sleep when you've got a baby.

Aged thirty-two, I had a miscarriage. I did not experience significant psychological distress, as I had already had a successful pregnancy and knew miscarriages were common. Nevertheless, the miscarriage was a sudden trigger, most likely due to the hormonal shifts it entails. After that I became severely unwell very rapidly, following much the same pattern as before. Outwardly calm, sociable and articulate, my internal world was a raging and speeding mess of intense agitation, euphoric visions, energy, disinhibition, and terrifying psychosis, all driving me inexorably towards suicide. The years which followed were a mess of failed treatments, multiple hospital admissions, 'sections', and numerous suicide attempts or near-attempts. As a 'revolving door' patient, I came very close to losing my life more than once, and am incredibly lucky to have survived without lasting injury. At one point, I found myself detained under the Mental Health Act and treated with ECT against my will. This was not at Northwick Park, but another hospital and with a different team. Things were badly mismanaged and, due to the misuse of benzodiazepines in close proximity to the ECT treatment, it was unsuccessful. The experience of forced ECT was extremely traumatic and I vowed that I would never have ECT again.

A couple of years later, I found myself at Northwick Park, under the care of an excellent team and a brilliant psychiatrist, who was determined not to give up on understanding what was wrong with me and how it could be treated. Despite my atypical presentation, he became convinced that I had bipolar disorder and, after a second opinion from a specialist bipolar team, I was diagnosed with bipolar I or, more precisely for me, Atypical Mixed Affective Disorder. Finally, I was introduced to the concept of a 'mixed state' and, after all these years, had an explanation which made sense of the cluster of often conflicting symptoms I experienced, together with the intense suicidality. Although we worked through all the conventional psychopharmacological (or 'drug') options for bipolar, nothing worked. Once again, my life was at risk and the psychiatrist, although he knew about my reluctance, suggested ECT. After analysing the medical records from the other hospital, people concluded that the ECT had been unsuccessful due to the heavy use of benzodiazepines in the 24-hour period prior to ECT. Despite many reservations, I agreed to try ECT again.

ECT worked just as it had worked in my twenties. The most severe symptoms were gone. Unfortunately, as I was now so fragile after many years of being unwell, I could not remain stable and experienced multiple relapses. ECT worked to alleviate the most severe symptoms and prevent the risk of suicide. But once the ECT was finished, it seemed that, within a few months, something would lead to me becoming unwell again.

Maintenance ECT

At this point, someone raised the possibility of maintenance ECT. ECT is a treatment which alleviates the most severe and life-threatening symptoms of mood disorder – but it's not a 'cure'. It gets people well enough that they can respond to other forms of treatment, whether that be psychological therapies or medication. For people who are 'treatment resistant' to these options, the months after ECT can be a difficult time, especially if ECT has been preceded by a lengthy period of illness, and the risk of relapse can be high. It was at this point, after multiple relapses, that both I and my clinical team looked into maintenance ECT. The picture looked optimistic. After an initial tapering period, maintenance ECT – or M-ECT, as it's sometimes known – can be carried out once a month, usually for a year to 18 months, sometimes longer; it's been shown to prevent relapse in people who seemed completely 'treatment resistant' and, for whom, like me, a continuous cycle of remission and relapse had become the norm. In addition, once the ECT treatments were spread out to once-monthly, not only would there be less disturbance from regular treatments, but the one side effect I had experienced – autobiographical memory loss – should subside.

For me, maintenance ECT was extremely successful. I had a course of approximately 16 months, during which time my health stabilised more than it had done for many years, and I was able to resume nearly all my normal functions. There were no cognitive side effects and life started to return to some type of normality. After I completed the course, I remained well for a good few years, so much so that we contemplated the possibility of trying for a second child – something which had seemed like an impossibility only two or three years beforehand, given that my health appeared so out of control, with no tangible signs of improvement.

I've had a course of maintenance ECT a couple of times since. I was severely unwell in the postnatal period and, after an acute course of ECT relieved the most severe symptoms, I had M-ECT for about a year to stabilise things. A couple of years later, due to a complex mix of hormonal and environmental triggers, I experienced another severe episode and repeated the same process. Each time, M-ECT has worked extremely well. It's got me through the difficult period which follows the initial relief of a severe episode subsiding, has not been arduous and has not resulted in any troublesome side effects. It has now been two years since I had my last M-ECT session. I know that I may relapse at some point, but so far I have stayed well.

Final Reflections on ECT

As no mood stabiliser has worked for me, the number of ECT treatments has mounted up over the years. I have now had ECT over 200 times. It hasn't been without any side effects. I have experienced autobiographical memory loss. This comes in the form of memory gaps, particularly around the time when I had an acute course of ECT. I've found ways to manage this specific form of localised amnesia and have written about it elsewhere. I do think that more could be done to recognise and research this phenomenon within the psychiatric research community. One research aspiration of mine is to run a study which gathers qualitative data from people who have had ECT about any experiences of long-term memory loss, with the hope of working towards better ways of assessing and managing this. I also had some negative experiences, a long time ago, where ECT was mismanaged by a poorly informed clinical team. I'm confident that there are much more stringent safeguards in place now.

The memory loss from ECT is very localised and restricted to short periods of my life. I can safely say that, after more than 200 treatments, I have not experienced any lasting cognitive decline or inability to build new memories. While receiving multiple rounds of ECT, I have managed to build a successful and fulfilling career as a researcher and lecturer.

Whilst severely and repeatedly unwell in my thirties, my academic career was on hold and, at the time, it seemed inconceivable that I would ever be well enough to return to that element of my life. Once stabilised through the M-ECT, I started to contact colleagues again and, through a series of strange coincidences, ended up working in the area of philosophy of medicine. Gradually, this shifted towards mental health ethics and law, and I found myself involved in everything from policy to clinical work. After a couple of years back at work, I became a Wellcome Trust Senior Research Fellow at the Institute of Psychiatry, Psychology and Neuroscience, King's College London. I jointly led a large research project on mental health advance directives, working with psychiatrists on the development and trial of clinical tools, and with policymakers, lawyers and bioethicists on ensuring that these clinical interventions could be practically and ethically translated into policy-based and legal changes.

It is now about twelve years since I changed direction in my work and I have a joint role, as the first Director of Research at the charity Bipolar UK and in an honorary capacity in the divisions of psychiatry at University College London and at Cardiff University.

There have been multiple publications, national and international conferences, lecturing and supervision, continuing input into national and international policy work, and a growing body of research, including work on ECT. During these same twelve years, I experienced multiple episodes of illness, and the courses of ECT and M-ECT which came before and after the birth of my younger daughter. Although I stopped working for a few months during the most severe stages of episodes of illness, in general, I managed to keep my roles going and continued with my work while receiving M-ECT.

If anything, it is the huge health benefits which ECT has brought me which have allowed me to get to a state of mental health where I can function in my professional role. To ECT and the teams who have administered it, I owe so much – my life, my family, my career. This may sound like some type of melodramatic hyperbole, but it is the truth.

8

A Lifelong Struggle through Depression and Madness
Liz's Story

Crow in flight. This is a vinyl cut print I created in 2018 of a crow that gave me 'signs' during my journey

My full scale 'madness' occurred four years after I had to retire as a doctor due to ill health – a result of my lifelong depression. Just shows that this terrible illness can happen to anyone, even us doctors. And in 2011, aged fifty-one, I discovered just how ill I had become . . .

Psychosis

My first psychotic beliefs began in 2011 when I attended a funeral. The deceased was the same age as my mother, and perhaps this was the trigger, because I began to believe that this was the practice run for my mother's funeral. Not long after, I went on a week's retreat to try to find some peace in my head. I knew I didn't want to be near people; instead, I walked alone for miles each day. And, on every walk, I saw things which I knew to be signs just for me: an albino peacock, a dead fox hanging from a tree, a piece of sheep's spine, a vole crossing my path. I tried to see the symbolism and the meaning in them all.

A few months later, I went away on a Welsh-speaking ladies' weekend. I remember being overwhelmed by the number of people there and retreated to be alone, becoming fascinated by a painting in one of the halls. The image appeared to me to be sexualised behaviour of soldiers during war. I felt it was a 'sign' for me regarding my past. I believed my grandfather's experiences in the First World War had passed sexual abuse down the generations to me, which I now know didn't happen at all.

It wasn't long after these feelings and visions that I was admitted to St Tydfil's hospital because my psychotherapist was concerned I had lost touch with reality. (I've had depression all my life and was seeing a psychotherapist by this point.) I remember the first day on the ward, pulling the curtain around my bed by the window, for protection. I also remember a nurse pulling it back in

8. A Lifelong Struggle through Depression and Madness

such a way that I felt as if it had ripped my skin off. That first night, I sat on my bed watching the sun go down and cried.

Life on the ward only seemed to increase my psychotic delusions. One patient asked me if I was a fake patient, which set me off on this idea. I started believing that the other patients on the ward were pretend patients, organised by the Maudsley Hospital (I had been offered a referral there once). A patient answered the phone in the office one day, saying 'Aberdare police station', so I believed he was an undercover policeman who was pretending to cut himself. Another thin female patient seemed normal to me, and I believed she was a psychologist, organising feedback sessions about my care with the other 'patients' from the Maudsley. I kept hiding in wardrobes and under my bed because I felt unsafe.

One night, when I couldn't sleep, I climbed on top of the pool table in the communal area and lay under my blanket, believing I was camping. Another time, I went into an empty, one-bedded room and hid in the wardrobe, believing it was a tree on the campsite. I was behaving bizarrely, particularly in the early hours of the morning. I was writing avidly in a book about my strange thoughts and experiences: for example, making lists of people who I thought had sexually abused me as a child. I believed the staff were involved in orgies on the floor above and felt I had to gather evidence to expose this.

No one attempted to try and appreciate why I was so frightened, or to understand my inner world. After a week, I gave a note to a psychiatrist, telling her 'they' were trying to kill me. I think, possibly, this was why I was moved to the psychiatric intensive care unit (PICU) shortly afterwards. In PICU my ideas got even worse. I remember two other patients – an old man with dementia and a woman with schizophrenia – who I believed were both plain-clothes police officers protecting me. I remember going into the smoking area with the woman, taking a drag of her cigarette and stubbing my arm with the hot ash. I would listen to the voices in my head telling me stories about supposed experiences in my childhood that hadn't happened in reality. I tried to escape, setting off the fire alarm twice, expecting the fire brigade to rescue me, as I believed there was a plot by the staff to kill me, to stop me whistleblowing about the orgies. The fire brigade and staff were not impressed. I also rang the police on many occasions, asking them to come and rescue me because someone was trying to kill me. I continued trying to hide in cupboards and under my bed. As a result, the door of the cupboard was bolted, the bed removed, and just a mattress left. When I tried to lock myself in my room, the staff broke the door down, held me down and injected me. The door was also removed. I felt more exposed than ever, and very frightened.

I remember avoiding sitting near the window at mealtimes in the lounge area, and ducking my head down, in case I got shot from outside. After ten days, my mother insisted on seeing me, complained to the doctor, and I was discharged from PICU. I remember being told that I was being sent 'upstairs' and I went mad, shouting because I thought I was going to be 'sacrificed' in the orgies.

I was discharged and spent time at my mother's house. I would often roam the streets in the surrounding area. I remember talking to various people I met along the road about the 'signs'. Some ignored me, some talked to me, and one woman shooed me away from her son. On one occasion, whilst following 'signs', I came to an ice cream van. I felt the instruction was to shout, 'I scream', as it sounded like 'ice cream'. I screamed as loud as I could and then fled to the public toilet and locked myself in. I was handcuffed and locked in a police cell for twenty-four hours. My mother was told that I was drunk. I believed I was being filmed. I hid under the mattress believing I was going back into the womb at eight months pregnancy. It felt like a cathartic experience, and the safest I'd ever felt.

8. A Lifelong Struggle through Depression and Madness

From the police cell I was readmitted to St Tydfil's psychiatric hospital. On two occasions I escaped via the fire door and ran away. I remember being returned by the police on one occasion after running barefoot, in pyjamas, in the rain, through the town.

At my request, I was discharged again. I refused to go home with my mother, who I did not believe was my mother. Eventually, I was persuaded I would be safe there for a few nights, but I arranged a DNA test to prove I was not related to her. I was advised to go to my GP for tablets, but behaved oddly, taking off my clothes in the GP's room. This time, the mental health services were not interested in admitting me to hospital. I ended up driving miles along the back roads of mid-Wales, arriving home late, to avoid being picked up by the police. Eventually, I left my car in Brecon and travelled by bus to mid-Wales. I managed to rent a bungalow near Dolgellau, miles away from home. I spent two weeks there, not sleeping much, experiencing nightmares and feeling anxious. I had panic attacks. I believed that my mother had died and that I had to hide for a year.

I spent each day walking the countryside, from early morning until the evening, following 'signs' that I believed had been put there to guide my trail. For example, I found a Nivea pearl lipstick on a bench and thought this was a message to keep smiling ... and that a group of ramblers from England were sent to comfort and encourage me. After I lost my wallet, the landlord called the police because of his concerns about me. I was admitted to hospital in Dolgellau but escaped the next morning.

My life of constant rambling through the countryside continued. I never took a map with me; I was following the 'signs'. These included things like a bus turning up, or a robin singing, telling me to stop, or a cow facing a certain way, guiding my direction as to where I should walk that day. When I got lost or unsure where to go, I would get stressed and angry, ranting at the jays, swearing and crying. The 'jays' were people I trusted, like my therapist, Jay. I believed they were guiding me with the various signs. Only once I did get really lost on a mountain and ended up in Harlech.

I usually had soaking wet feet from walking in boggy land and bought myself another pair of walking shoes in Aberystwyth, as my feet were blistered. I had to spend some time each evening washing my clothes in the machine and then my shoes by hand. The washing machine confused me as I felt any instructions should be reversed.

I ended up trying to drown myself in the river, as felt that the 'team' protecting and guiding me had abandoned me. I floated in my clothes, but got out again, crawling up on the bank. I was eventually picked up by ambulance and taken to Aberystwyth Hospital. Once again, I was discharged, to a local B&B, and told to wait for a social worker the next morning, but I left at 6:30am. I was later arrested for shoplifting as I had no money and was cold and hungry. I spent the day in a police cell, shouting and swearing and banging the windows with frustration. I was later seen by the mental health team and taken by a police van to a unit in Haverfordwest. On the first day in the hospital I smashed up the furniture in my room. I tried to escape the unit several times, twice by climbing over the fence, and once was escorted back by police after screaming and squirting beauty products at the shoppers in a store. After two days I was taken back to Merthyr in the evening and discharged immediately.

My mother took me to her home in Cardiff, but I could not settle to sleep so she took me back to my home in Merthyr. Once there, we went to bed. However, I got up, locked her in, took her car and drove around, sleeping the night in a car park. The next day, before sunrise, I drove up a one-way street in Neath while following my 'signs' and was stopped by police and taken to the hospital. I escaped and threw stones at cars in the car park, believing it was a film set organised for me to vent my anger. I broke several car windows before being caught and taken by police to a local mental health unit. I was then sent back to St Tydfil's PICU and sectioned. My diagnosis was changed to psychogenic psychosis. I was started on medications: quetiapine and clonazepam.

Finally, my journey into madness came to an end and I was treated for psychosis. Whilst back in PICU, the staff treated me better than the first time. I was moved to another ward and felt much happier with the staff approach. After two months I was discharged and supported by a community psychiatric nurse, and later by a social worker. She supported me to obtain Disabled Student Allowance for a BA arts degree. Looking back, I realise the incredible strain and sacrifice my mother endured during these three months of madness.

I wrote a few poems about my psychotic experiences; here is one of them, called 'Messages':

Psychosis: Messages

The robin stopped me in my tracks with his shrill song.
'Look' he seemed to say, 'you've missed a vital sign':
A finger post pointing the way,
that Welsh black bull sat down ahead,
those mountains in all their glory.
And when the torrent of river drowned out birdsong,
a beech leaf falling on the path,
or the wind changing direction spoke to me.

A woman sat in her window looking down as I passed,
as if she understood I needed to slip by unnoticed.
A horse nuzzled me along in the right directions,
while the chaotic movement of sheep
often left me confused.
Crows cackled in mockery when I missed a cue.
Jays chattered in the trees as if sharing confidences,
reassuring me I was cared for, guided,
although the way remained a mystery to me.

At night, lying in bed, the house shifted and
groaned in answer to my questions.
My stomach rumbled in communication.
I was wakened by dreams and nightmares,
immediately alert to their coded messages.

I followed obediently, beating myself up
when I was chided for getting it wrong.
At times I could barely breathe with fear
or wept at my losses or raged at the mess
YOU had left in me.

My restless mind tried to assimilate the barrage of information.
Sharing my thoughts and feelings was forbidden.
All I knew was that I had to avoid being caught
and Christmas was significant in some way.
I must keep my head down
and just move on to the year's end.
Second guessing wasn't going to help.
Clarity would come later.

But when the man passed me that day
holding his hands close to his chest
I snapped, wading into the water,
thinking of Virginia Woolf
and wishing I had her courage.

Childhood

I believe that the roots of my depression are to be found in my childhood. My father died when I was only two-and-a-half years old, following a second heart attack. He was only thirty-six years old. As I was so young, I remember very little about him. My only memory of him is when he smacked me and took me down from a stool in the hall when I was flicking the light switch on and off. While recovering from the heart attack in a rehabilitation hospital, he made me a wicker basket in occupational therapy, which I still treasure. He also made a rug which I have in my house. A close friend of my mother once told me that he and I were inseparable.

After my father's death, I remember my mother crying in the toilet. I tried to go in, to find out what was happening. She closed the door on me to keep me out. She worked as a secretary until she retired aged sixty-three. She prided herself on never missing a day's work, and in the early years she used to cycle to work. Perhaps we didn't spend much time together, as she had to spend her time providing for the family after my father had died. I loved playing with my dolls and still love them. I suppose it was not just my father's absence from my life, but also the effect his death had on my mother that may have caused problems during my childhood. Looking back, I had some problems with my mood and confidence from an early age. When I was very young, I used to avoid going to the toilet until it became extremely painful to go and I would be crying. I suppose there was some connection with me being unhappy. I was taken to see a paediatrician at the hospital. This was a traumatic experience as two men were looking at my bottom to find out if there was anything wrong.

When I was eleven, after a course of antibiotics for boils on my stomach, I had problems swallowing. I was seen by the paediatrician who noticed, on the chest X-ray, that I had a right-sided aorta. I was referred to a professor in cardiology who arranged for me to have a cardiac catheterisation. I was admitted at the end of the summer holidays for three days and had to miss Guide camp. The procedure itself was uncomfortable as I felt the cannula poking my blood vessels. The following day I complained of pain in my right foot. I was diagnosed with an embolus and started on a heparin drip. I was most excited to have a drip like my friend in the bed opposite, without realising how serious my condition was. I ended up staying in for ten days and started secondary school late, which I found challenging.

When I returned home from hospital in September 1971, I found that the man from across the road, Mac, was at my house, and discovered my mother was having an affair. I told her I did not want him there and she told me 'Hard cheddar, I love him.' I felt rejected. Mac visited us regularly and came to live with us in 1973 when we moved house.

As a child I had a stutter and was very shy. I remember the shame I felt when I stuttered through the Brownie promise in front of our parents. When I was in secondary school, I still had a speech impediment. I used to dread English classes when we had to read from a novel in turn. I would stutter and struggle to get my words out.

When I was thirteen, I was entered into an inter-school's cross-country race. I came third and came home with a plaque. I remember how I overtook the trainer's daughter at the finish sprint. I was very proud of how I did, and of the plaque. My mother made no comment about it when I got home, and I remember being disappointed at her lack of interest. She did, however, allow me to join the local athletics club and bought me a pair of Gola trainers. I used to train at Maindy Stadium twice a week and run in races every Saturday. I had to walk the two miles home after a race, because nobody gave me a lift back home. I never slept well on Saturday nights as I would get cramps in my legs. In the summer, we ran in track races: 800 and 1,500 metres and later 3,000 metres. I remember one sports day at school, I won all the track races, including 100, 200, 400, 800 and 1,500 metres. I continued to run twice a week until my admission to hospital in April 2022. I still run these days, well into my sixties. I recently entered for the Crickhowell 10K run, when I will be sixty-four.

When I was fifteen, my stepfather, Mac, left my mother and went back to his wife. My mother went to pieces. Although she continued to work, at home she was depressed and cried all the time. Her friends told me to look after her. Mac came back later when I wrote to him at my mother's request.

8. A Lifelong Struggle through Depression and Madness

During one of the summer school holidays, aged seventeen, I went to volunteer in a children's home. I took a small overdose of paracetamol, but didn't tell anybody, just went to sleep. Looking back, I think this may have been when I was first depressed, but I didn't realise it at the time. My schoolwork deteriorated but, thankfully, it picked up by the time I took my A levels, and I got two As and a B.

I had always wanted to be a children's nurse, but I remember my biology teacher encouraging me to think of being a children's doctor. So, I applied to do medicine. Mum insisted I went away to university, and so I travelled to Liverpool. I remember the first time my mother took me up to the hall of residence. When we arrived at halls, Mum produced a box with tea and coffee and chocolate biscuits, etcetera, and I was touched by her care. I was in halls for two years and made some good friends, who I am still in touch with today. I went on my student elective to the Edinburgh Medical Missionary Society hospital in Nazareth.

Back at home, I discovered my stepfather had left my mother when he was made redundant, taking his redundancy money with him. She was more angry than depressed this time.

Depression

I was first given a diagnosis of depression, and started on antidepressants, in my fourth year of Medicine, aged twenty-two. I had been doing an attachment to a GP for four weeks. The GP thought I was depressed and referred me to the sub-dean, who was a psychiatrist. The sub-dean was horrible to me, telling me I should have known I was depressed and should have diagnosed myself, but I hadn't done psychiatry and didn't know I was suffering with depression! I was referred to my own GP for medication, and he started me on the antidepressant imipramine.

In my final year, I applied to the Welsh rotation for my house jobs as I wanted to be near my mother. I moved to Merthyr Tydfil to do my pre-registration jobs in 1983. Following this, I did my GP training in Merthyr. The obstetrics rota was particularly hard as I was on call every other day and would often get called, in error, on my night off. I then became a GP in the town in 1987. In 1993 I moved jobs to work for the child and adolescent psychiatry service. I became increasingly interested in Family Therapy and was able to attend Family Therapy conferences in Glasgow, Oslo and Israel as part of my education.

I struggled with depression on and off over the years, trying various antidepressants. They either had no effect or gave me unpleasant side effects, most commonly symptoms of activation. I continued to exercise, mostly running, and even managed to run the London Marathon in 1994. I did a lot of half marathons, once finishing first Merthyr lady. Running keeps me sane.

After working for nearly twenty years, I was taking longer spells of leave. I was referred for a second opinion in 2005 and saw Dr Kirov. We counted at least ten antidepressants that had been tried over the years. I had also tried lithium, which caused irritability and sleep problems. It was clear that drugs caused side effects for me, and I couldn't tolerate the usual full doses. Dr Kirov suggested several options, including monoamine oxidase inhibitors and another mood stabiliser. These changes were tried over the next few years but didn't bring any relief.

In 2005, I was off work for ten months and, at that time, started seeing a psychotherapist privately. Despite all the antidepressants, the psychotherapy, and regular exercise, in 2007 I made the decision to retire on grounds of ill health. I continued seeing my psychotherapist for four and a half years until she retired. When she retired in 2010, my psychiatrist referred me to see a psychotherapist under the NHS. In psychotherapy we addressed early childhood hurts such as my father dying suddenly when I was two and a half and the relationship I had with my mother. The psychotherapist felt that I had had an emotionally avoidant childhood in that my mother was critical, showed little interest and never expressed her love physically or verbally. I worked with this psychotherapist for about eighteen months then she suddenly resigned, leaving me devastated.

ECT

After retiring, I started a course in art and gained a BA after two years at Merthyr College. I was still prone to ups and downs and anxiety, but settled on a good dose of various medications, with the usual side effects. And then, in 2011 the months of madness mentioned above happened and took over my life ...

After this period, life was better, but towards the end of 2014 things once again became more stressful as my mother developed a haematoma which later became an ulcer. She was in so much pain and it wasn't healing, eventually requiring a below-the-knee amputation. My mood was going down again. After more unsuccessful medication trials, I was seen by Professor Kirov again, in 2016. The episode of psychosis in 2011 made him change his diagnosis to bipolar disorder. We counted that by now I had been tried on eighteen different antidepressants and six mood stabilisers. He suggested that I stop making changes and remain on what seemed to be suiting me best.

In 2021 I was readmitted twice with depression: in January and in March. I was offered ECT, but this didn't happen as the ECT psychiatrist and anaesthetist had retired and so ECT was no longer available in my area.

My mother was in hospital in April 2021 and came home with a pressure sore on her buttock. From this time on, she received double-handed visits four times a day. Initially, she was lifted from chair to bed or commode by hoist, which she hated. She would often refuse personal care. She finally became confined to her bed downstairs.

In April 2022 I was admitted to the Royal Glamorgan Hospital with severe treatment-resistant depression. Professor Kirov came to see me in the hospital. I must have looked pretty depressed, as he suggested starting ECT at Llandough Hospital. He noted that I looked worse than on previous occasions, and that I showed 'psychomotor agitation' that gave some hope that ECT could work, even after all the other treatments had failed. He did point out that, with such a long history of depression, my chances of getting better were not that good. I found the suggested 40 per cent chance of improvement rather low, but I felt quite desperate so decided to go ahead, even after the warning of potential memory problems, other side effects and the possible need to carry on with ECT for some time after I improved. My mother pleaded with me not to have ECT. She was in tears, frightened it would change my personality. It was so hard, I felt guilty.

The following week I started ECT and initially had it twice weekly, then weekly, fortnightly, etcetera. The first time, I felt nervous as I had never had general anaesthetic before, let alone a fit! After the first session I felt really rough, especially with nausea. I was given medication for this but still felt the same. I was OK for the first two hours, apart from painful jaw muscles, but then I felt terrible, lying in bed but not sleeping. The next day I felt a lot better, but still not 100 per cent. The second time, I didn't feel as sick. After the sixth session, I messaged a friend, telling her that I felt better. She kept visiting me in the hospital regularly and, after the eighth session, she told me that I looked so much better. I improved a lot and was discharged on 15th June 2022, after a total of thirteen sessions. My memories from that time are blurred, and I struggle to give more details of the treatment, but everyone tells me that I was really well.

My improvement didn't last long. My mother, now aged ninety-five, had been bed-bound for many months and I had visited her,

8. A Lifelong Struggle through Depression and Madness

at her home in Cardiff, every Saturday while I was in hospital. On the final Saturday I visited, she was admitted to Llandough Hospital with sepsis in her pressure sores. I was still having ECT and visited her on the Tuesday, after my ECT. I was discharged on the next day and planned to come back and visit her again in the hospital on the Friday. However, she died at 5:30am that day.

Unsurprisingly, any improvement I had with my mood fell away, and has not really picked up since, despite continuing with ECT. My relationship with my mother had improved in later years, particularly after seeing her concern for me during my admission for psychosis in 2011. I do find happiness and some form of healing from the telephone conversation we had during her final week, when I told her I loved her, and she told me she loved me. I miss my mother so much.

I was an executor of her will, so had to arrange the funeral and empty my mother's house. Just emptying one of my mother's wardrobes one day left me emotionally drained. I then had to sell the house and find accommodation for my older brother, who lived with my mother. This added to the stress, and I slipped back into depression, which hasn't fully lifted since even with ECT. We decided not to increase the sessions to twice per week as my memory was already becoming a problem and I didn't want to make it worse. For example, it took me an hour to tune the channels on my TV at home, as I couldn't remember how to use the two handsets and, even then, I couldn't get BBC2.

Today, I have no interest in former activities like art or gardening. I need to sleep a lot, going to bed at 6-7pm, reading for an hour, then going to sleep. I sometimes wake up in the night and can't get back to sleep for ages. I still take 1mg clonazepam at night and find I need this to get to sleep.

I continue to have maintenance ECT at intervals of four weeks. I have now had more than forty ECTs over a period of two years. I am taken by taxi from my home in Merthyr to Llandough

Hospital, which takes an hour and a quarter. Our local hospital had an ECT clinic, but it was closed a few years ago and this treatment was taken over by the Cardiff clinic. The staff in the ECT unit are lovely and the process is efficient. The consultant is always in the room, which I find reassuring. I drift off to sleep easily with the general anaesthetic. I usually fully wake up in a chair in the post-recovery room with my shoes back on. I am given toast and tea and, once I am fine, I am taken home by taxi. In the afternoon I usually go to bed for a couple of hours and doze or sleep before getting up for tea. When I go to sleep in the night I tend to sleep very well and deeply. Since starting the ECT I have very vivid dreams.

Memory Loss

My main concern has been the effect of ECT on my memory. Both my long-term and short-term memory have been affected. People talk about things I did years ago with them, and I don't remember. I friend of mine had a mastectomy six years ago. She recently told me that I visited her every week after the operation, but I don't remember it. I also have problems remembering things that happened a few weeks ago. I sometimes have difficulty spelling words and struggle with arithmetic. I find it hard to find my way to places I've been to in the past and rely on Google maps more. I can't visualise places when people talk about them, even though I know I've been there before. I went jogging with a friend recently and she said that we did the route two weeks ago, but I had no memory of it. When reading novels, I find I cannot remember the plot or a character that reappears. I also have no memory of the Covid-19 pandemic and lockdown. I have difficulty remembering people's names. I sometimes get muddled with dates despite keeping a diary. Recently, I was supposed to meet a friend from

8. A Lifelong Struggle through Depression and Madness

Hereford in Hay on Wye, but instead went to Cardiff for my car service a day early. I was mortified to have dragged my friend to Hay and not turn up, as I am usually a reliable person who arrives on time.

When writing my narrative of psychiatric experiences, I relied on notes and letters taken at the time. I have no memory of being off work in 2005, seeing Dr G in 2009, Dr Kirov in 2005 or being admitted to Royal Glamorgan Hospital in 2021. Apparently, in 2016, I took my wheelchair-bound mother to the Isle of Man for her ninetieth birthday. I have no memory of this.

My friends say I am better, compared to when I went into hospital, but I still feel low and, at times, wish I was dead. I need to ring the emergency mental health service on 111 when I am very low. It helps to talk to the mental health worker. My friends say I should stop ECT because of the effect on my memory, but I am so scared of relapsing. I regularly discuss the memory problems with my doctor. They tried to change to right unilateral ECT, to reduce the problem, but my mood deteriorated and it wasn't possible to give me the required electric charge, as I was already on a high dose, probably due to the clonazepam. At the end of these discussions, I always decide to continue with ECT.

What moved me was my friend telling me how much improved she felt I was when she visited me in hospital after I started ECT, although she saw a drop in my mood after my mother's death. Her eyes filled with tears as she remembered how I had been before ECT. And, in church, one lady came up to me and said I'd come so far in the last year and was unrecognisable.

I know that I am not completely well right now, but, despite the memory loss, I feel I am a little better with ECT and am scared to stop it in case of further relapse. This fear never leaves me.

[Liz completed her 10 k run in the summer of 2024. Shortly after that, she decided to stop the maintenance ECT due to her memory problems.]

9

Rollercoaster – My Ride from Suicide to Survival
Berlinda's Story

9. Rollercoaster: My Ride from Suicide to Survival

Still to this day, I don't know why it happened. I was in a loving marriage, didn't have major financial problems, with a successful (if stressful) career. I had a few worries about loved ones and friends, but no more than everyone experiences, I suppose. It sounds strange to say, but my condition began to worsen significantly after I had taken two holidays in quick succession during 2018: the first to Las Vegas, to scatter my father-in-law's ashes, and then to Spain for a weekend to celebrate my own father's seventy-fifth birthday. You would imagine that taking these breaks would have reduced any stress and discomfort I had. Instead, it was at that point that my husband began to notice my mood swinging dramatically, and some issues with my sleeping and interacting with other people and family members. My job has always been in customer services; being relaxed and getting on with people has been second nature to me, so he could see how closed off I was becoming. You must understand that no one, not even I, realised how bad this was going to get. We all live in a state of hope: hope that you'll get better, hope that you'll start to recover. This was not just like a switch being flicked and suddenly I'm suicidal; this was a slow and inexorable descent which nobody could have expected or predicted.

My husband used to joke that, if sleeping was an Olympic sport, I'd win a gold medal. So, when I started to have trouble dropping off and was getting up earlier and earlier, he really began to worry. Later, the whole family beat themselves up, saying that we should have been more aware of the signs and been more receptive to helping before things got a lot worse, but we all have 20/20 vision in hindsight. And things did get worse . . . . . .

In October 2018, I attempted to take my life on numerous occasions; the first time was by trying to run into traffic, which led to my family ensuring the house was secure and not allowing me to go anywhere on my own. In retrospect, this could not have done the psychosis I developed any good – to be basically locked up – but what could they do? We managed to get a meeting with my local GP, and I can remember driving to the surgery with my husband and mum in the car and realising that I had to pull over because I was having thoughts of crashing it. That's the weird thing: I was ready to end my own life, but I didn't want to harm those I loved in the process. The doctor prescribed sleeping tablets, in the hope that a good night's sleep might help, but the thoughts in my head would still keep me up at night. About a week later, I was able to smuggle the keys away from whoever had them (who would have thought that paranoia would unlock my latent larceny skills!). I rushed out of the house, jumped into the car and reversed off the drive, straight into a van that had no chance of avoiding me, and drove away, with no idea of what I was doing. I only managed to make it about 500 yards down the road before I hit another car and ended up crashing into a skip by the local golf course. People were soon gathering around the car, asking me if I was OK or needed an ambulance, but I just sat there in a state of shock. I have no memory of this, but my husband and brother soon arrived and were there when the inevitable blue flashing lights showed up.

Even now I am amazed and feel very fortunate that I didn't hurt anyone else. Of course, at this point, with the police being involved, perhaps my family should have pushed for admission to a psychiatric hospital, but they were ever the optimists and still hoped that I would get better surrounded by their love and affection. Between these incidents, I had been prescribed Prozac (an antidepressant) and was given it every day along with the evening sleeping tablets so, perhaps, the hope was that at some point the medication would kick in and start to help me. Little did they know that I was saving these Prozac pills with the intention of taking an overdose. If I had saved the sleeping tablets, and taken them all in one go, I'm sure I wouldn't be here now. My only thought was that I still wanted to get a good night's sleep, so I wouldn't run the risk of not taking a sleeping tablet each night.

In early November, I must have decided I had got enough Prozac saved up in a sock beside our bed and took them all. It was, probably, the most peaceful and relaxed I had felt in months, so I climbed into bed next to my husband and curled up with my head on his chest. It must have been such a change to see me relaxed and not manic that he soon realised something was 'off'. He asked me what had happened, and why I was so chilled out; I told him about the tablets I had just taken, and suddenly the house was a lot less calm and relaxed. An ambulance was called, I was kept on my feet walking around the bedroom and eventually rushed off to A&E. Possibly far later than they should have, my husband and brothers decided that there was no way that they could keep me safe at home, and a hospital ward was the only secure place where I could be looked after. As soon as I was given the 'all clear' that not enough medication had entered my system, it was all hands on deck to try and find a bed in a psychiatric hospital. The mental health nurse at A&E made it abundantly clear that there were no beds on the local wards and, even after she had rung around other units, the soonest they could get me admitted would be Monday morning. At that point, it was Friday night. My family spent the next few hours frantically trying anywhere for a bed; even private facilities had no availability, and they were facing another spell of trying to look after me over the weekend. My family always say that when the mental health nurse came, in the early hours of Saturday morning, to say that a bed was available at the local psychiatric unit, it felt like nothing short of a miracle.

I've been told what happened on the night when I was admitted to the ward. I was banging my head against a table, whilst shouting and screaming at the nurses who would come in. My reaction was possibly due to my annoyance – the realisation that I'd have less chance to kill myself if I was locked up. Who knows? The admissions nurse explained that I would be held on a temporary order, but this, eventually, could be extended to a Section 2. Little did I know that this would be my home for the next six months – barring a short stay in Oldham General, but we'll get to that later.

It's hard to describe how I was feeling during the time on the ward. Although you are there for treatment and safety, you're also surrounded by other patients with a wide variety of conditions and some of my fellow patients did not help my paranoid fixations at all. I can remember little; interactions with patients and staff were very difficult as I was convinced that everyone was there to spy on me, and I scribbled notes that I would pass to my family at visits. I have since seen some of these notes and cannot decipher the incoherent ramblings – they are so foreign to me that I feel they were written by someone else. I have also taken the opportunity to read through my hospital notes. The key 'theme' for me was the noises in my head. Notes repeatedly say I was sat with my head in my hands. My head was full of thoughts and the noise was overwhelming and overpowering. The first time this happened was when I was having a takeaway with the family (my husband, two brothers and mum), but I was distant and unaware of all the activity around me as my head was so full of noise. It was like I was looking in on everyone talking and eating but I was invisible, with a head full of noise!

The overwhelming delusion at that point was that I needed to be humiliated or punished (for what, I still don't know). There was an upcoming boxing event around that time in Manchester and I was absolutely convinced that the hospital staff were going to put me in a straitjacket, bring me out into the ring between rounds and show the world how crazy I was. I can't remember what excuse I gave to any visitor when this event came and went without me being rolled out in front of the cameras, but I'm sure it was absolutely justifiable in my mind. I was also able to see the very slight errors that had been put into TV shows and adverts that meant they were made especially to taunt or threaten me.

Yet, every time my husband or family came to visit, I tried to make it abundantly clear that I didn't want to hurt them in the slightest and that I just needed to quieten the voices in my head. I knew that none of these drugs, treatments or therapies were ever going to work because the voices were real, and they were right.

During this time, I was put on numerous different medications, none of which had any significant impact on my mental well-being. But after a month or so on the ward, I was allowed accompanied leave with nurses or family. During one particularly fraught afternoon out to a local coffee shop with my husband and father, I became severely agitated and was banging my head against the table whilst screaming and shouting that I didn't want to go back to the ward. After much gentle persuasion and comforting, I eventually got back in the car and was driven back to the ward, with my husband holding on to me so that I couldn't try to leap out of the moving vehicle. However, even after explaining to the staff how worried they were about my state of mind, and that unaccompanied leave should perhaps be postponed, the following day I was allowed out of the ward for my first fifteen minutes of unaccompanied leave.

As I said, my memories of this time are fuzzy at best, and much of this information comes from recollections shared with me by my friends and family. Most patients, when they are allowed out, with or without a chaperone, usually take the opportunity to smoke a cigarette or just get some fresh air and a bit of a break from the confines of the ward. On my first unaccompanied leave I knew exactly what I was going to do. I immediately walked out of the hospital grounds to the adjacent major road. I sat there for some time, watching the cars rush by, my mind churning over what was happening. Did I consider what my death would do to my family? I suppose I must have but, eventually, the noise in my mind drowned out every rational thought, and I ran out between parked cars in front of an oncoming vehicle. I don't know if I was just lucky, or if the driver had fantastic reactions. I ended up with a leg broken in three places, but I was still alive. The ambulance must have arrived in minutes (I suppose that's one benefit of trying to kill yourself in front of a major hospital!), but I was convinced that the gentleman who stayed with me, and I presume who called the ambulance, was a paid actor and that I would be taken in the ambulance to be hidden away in a basement somewhere. Even the pain of having my leg broken was not enough to silence those damn voices in my head.

The ambulance driver rang my husband to explain what had happened, and said that they were taking me to another hospital as the one I was staying in didn't have a trauma unit. My husband clearly remembers hearing my voice in the background telling him that they were going to hide me away somewhere and he should be glad that he would never see or hear from me again.

When I arrived at A&E, a quick X-ray examination showed how badly my leg was broken and I was rushed into theatre for my leg to be pinned and an external fixator cage fitted. It was at this point that I was guarded twenty-four hours a day by nurses assigned from the mental health ward, with one watching over me continuously in eight-hour shifts. It's likely that this level of supervision actively increased my paranoia and, after a couple of days, despite the fixator cage on my leg, I managed to crawl out of bed when the nurse went for a toilet break. I don't know where the hell I thought I was going, or how I was going to get anywhere, but I just needed to get out of that ward. When the nurse returned, I was thrashing about on the floor, trying to crawl whilst dragging my caged leg behind me, powered on by sheer desperation. I had to be held down by about six doctors and nurses, causing numerous injuries to the staff who were trying to stop me from hurting myself even further. Remember that, at this point, I was on a trauma unit, not a mental health ward, so the staff were not trained to deal with such acute mania. I can't even begin to think what the other patients on the ward must have thought:

they were probably worried for their own safety. But I knew that they were all actors and that the radio in the ward was set up to torment me. There was even a constant drip of my favourite perfume from the ceiling tile above me, but they had done something so that every time it dripped on my skin, it burned like acid. These poor doctors and nurses, and I think a couple of physiotherapists, were holding me for at least an hour until my husband turned up and was able to calm me down enough for them to lift me back into the bed.

Pretty soon after that incident, the hospital got me into theatre and a full operation was needed to insert further pins into my leg and remove the fixator cage. As soon as I had recovered enough from the surgery, I was back in an ambulance to the mental health unit. So, coming up to Christmas 2018, I was back on the ward with my Section 2 extended to a Section 3, which is valid for up to six months, and even more paranoid about the staff and patients. It also didn't help that my mobility was limited due to being in a wheelchair, and I felt that they were torturing me by getting me up to practice walking to improve my mobility. It's hard to motivate yourself to exercise and get better when you're convinced that the world wants you gone.

There were very few times when I felt any glimpse of happiness during the winter of 2018. Some visits from family or friends would find me angry or tearful, and my husband can clearly recall the time when I told him that he shouldn't come to visit any more as I was never going to get better. More medications were tried, and the dosages varied, to try and elicit any sort of improvement in me, to no avail. It was even suggested that I may have been pretending to take the tablets (due to the total lack of impact) and I was instead prescribed injections. The family and I had weekly meetings with the doctors and other clinicians to discuss how my treatment was going and what the options were. Every three weeks another treatment plan would be suggested, and my family would get hope that this would be the answer. Of course, I knew that nothing was going to help, simply because I was damaged beyond repair.

It was probably towards the end of January 2019 that the idea of ECT was first mentioned to me and my family at a multi-disciplinary team meeting. I think the reason I did not argue or try to dismiss this treatment, despite its negative image, was simply that nothing else had worked, so my paranoia was convincing me that this wouldn't work either. My family were also sceptical about the ECT, but were more reassured after talking with my consultant and by the research my brother did on this subject. Both advised that, although the reasons behind the benefits were not clear, the simple fact that it had significantly helped many people in exactly my situation was more than enough reason to try.

There was still a worry that I would change my mind and decide not to consent to undergo ECT. But, on Monday 25th February 2019, I signed the consent form and was taken over to the elective treatment rooms for the first of twelve sessions. I can't remember anything about any of the treatments. The overwhelming feeling when I came out from the anaesthetic was of being refreshed. My husband was told that there was no point coming back that Monday evening at visiting hours as I would be sleeping most of the time due to the treatment and the anaesthetic wearing off.

As fate would have it, the Tuesday after my first treatment was my husband's birthday and he still says that it was the greatest birthday present he's ever had; that, after being buzzed into the ward, I saw him, gave him a big smile, stood up from my wheelchair and gave him a hug. Tears still well up in his eyes when he tells me that story. He also makes a point that, for the first time since I was admitted, I made him a cup of coffee, which we had with a slice of birthday cake he'd brought in. That evening was the first time he saw a glimpse of the person I used to be.

Everyone says the change in me was almost immediate: from being confrontational and abusive with the staff, patients and other visitors, to starting to engage with everyone. As I said, my job is in the hospitality sector, so I've never had any problem with talking and getting on with people, and now they were finally able to see the real me. I still had moments of darkness, but they were few and far between, and they became even rarer as my treatments, every Monday and Thursday, progressed. There were even things I actually started to enjoy on the ward, like the fresh toast with loads of butter on that they made for supper. And, even though the other patients were still suffering with their own problems, I stopped seeing them as actors and started to see them as people with their own mental health issues. Visits from family and friends would now find me playing cards with other patients, chatting with them and the staff, reading and even helping out on the ward if I could.

It was probably after four sessions of ECT that I was, once again, granted leave from the ward, initially with family out for a coffee and snack, but then, eventually, unaccompanied. My family were understandably worried about this, but nowhere near to the same level as before I had my accident. During this unaccompanied leave, I would often take requests from other patients on the ward to pick them up newspapers, cigarettes, or snacks from the garage down the road – the same road that I had run out into less than three months earlier. I don't remember how I felt being so close to the place I had such a traumatic experience. If I'm being honest, a lot of the memories I have from my 'bad' time feel like they were someone else's; it feels like I am writing about something that happened to a character in a film I watched or a book that I had read.

My treatments were stopped after the tenth session as it was felt that I had benefited from the ECT as much as I could. So, in early April, I also got a fantastic birthday present myself when my consultant signed to discharge me from the hospital and I was able to curl up in my own bed for the first time in six months. It's still strange, thinking back on all that time of the slow deterioration, the suicide attempts, the absolute conviction that I was never going to get well, and comparing that with the person I am now. If I was hearing the story from someone else, I'd be amazed that someone could be so low and lose all hope of recovery, and then a simple procedure could make such a dramatic change.

I wish I knew why the ECT works; maybe it was just a trigger to allow my brain to let the medications do their work (and I am still on these medications, although in much smaller doses), but it has given me back my life and, although I have made a lot of changes to look after my mental health, I credit the ECT with giving me the chance to get better. I will admit that I have some gaps in my memory about my time of being ill and being on the ward, but nobody can convince me that these weren't due to the medications, the mania or even the environment that I found myself in for six months of my life.

Following my mental health rollercoaster, I am now an advocate for ECT and work with the Royal College of Psychiatrists as a Patient Representative for the ECT Accreditation Service (ECTAS), reviewing clinics for adhering to their standards. I also work with the Patient Advisory Liaison Service (PALS) and I am due to start working with second-year medical students, teaching within 'Patients as Educators' and informing them of my ECT journey.

But my biggest change has simply been to embrace those things that give you pleasure, and not put them off. Before I got ill, my husband and I had always talked about getting a dog, but the time never felt right. As I write this, I've got one big furry beauty curled up around my feet and another fast asleep on the sofa next to me. We were also fortunate enough to find an amazing house in the countryside with a lot more land to enjoy – although I don't know how I didn't have a relapse with the stress of moving! Even though I went through all those ups and downs, I know I'm luckier than most, as I could have succeeded in one of my suicide attempts or I could have hurt someone or chosen not to have ECT. But I'm here and I'm happy, and, in all honesty, it's not a bad place to be.

To sum up: Oct 2018 to date – WHAT A RIDE!!!!!

10

The Doll's House
Sue's Story

From the perspective of many, I was living a charmed life: financially secure, a stable and supportive marriage, a holiday home and lots of vacations as a result of early retirement. I hadn't planned on retiring as early as I did – fifty-six is too young to be on the shelf, and I had planned to taper off my working life. I was a freelance social worker offering a range of services to local authorities; chairing reviews of children's care plans, as well as chairing child protection conferences, was my bread and butter. I was very busy and received a lot of positive feedback, therefore retirement wasn't something to look forward to. Unfortunately, local-authority policy changes meant that freelancers were no longer used, so I either had to go back into full-time employment or stop altogether. As most vacancies were already filled, my workload dwindled until there was nothing. I toyed with the idea of going back in-house, but was in the fortunate position to be able to decide not to. So, after thirty plus years there was no celebration of my rite of passage, just quite an abrupt ending with no plan in place for retirement.

In March 2020 Covid-19 struck. We had been at our home in Spain for two months, and I needed to come home as the MOT was due on my car. Having decided that there was no need for both of us to travel, my husband, James, stayed in Spain and I flew back, expecting to be back in Spain a week later. I even planned to bring a couple of friends as guests at our Spanish home. The following Monday, after the flight home to Wales, I started coughing and duly self-isolated for seven days. On the same day Spain went into a very strict lockdown – my husband was only permitted to go to the local shop, all flights ceased and the ferries would only accept bookings for freight. We had no idea that we would be locked down in separate countries for four months; like most people, we thought that the lockdowns would only be for a few weeks. In the event, it was mid-July before I was able to return to Spain and be reunited with my husband. We had a few days of very restricted 'holiday' at

10. The Doll's House

the coast before returning to our Spanish home, then, a few weeks later, we were able to drive back to Cardiff. I continued to experience periodic episodes of burning lungs, which I believe were Covid symptoms, and they lasted until September of that year.

Possibly because of these factors and events, I began to feel very anxious and suicidal. I hadn't previously had any history of mental health problems apart from a brief episode in my thirties following a relationship breakdown. I was prescribed medication by my GP but, in December 2020, I took my first overdose, sparked by the belief that I could not access my new mobile phone and computer. I took prescribed medication as well as a few paracetamols. My husband took me to A&E, but I have no recollection of what happened. He tells me that I was kept in overnight, and then sent home following an assessment by the psychiatrist attached to A&E.

The anxiety and suicidal thoughts developed into psychosis. I was convinced that my phone and computer were connecting to the dark web and that, in some way, I was undermining the country's child protection system by infecting it with computer viruses. I even contacted my sister-in-law, who is also a very senior social worker, to warn her that she might be implicated. This was terrifying for me. I was also becoming convinced that my husband no longer wanted to be with me, that he had another woman and that he was going to cheat me out of my money. I also believed that I would not be paid my local authority pension. I did not believe his denials and, even when he found documentary evidence that my pension would be paid, I developed the belief that the paperwork related to somebody else with the same name and national insurance number. Believing that I would become destitute and homeless, I had a bag packed and I was talking about sleeping on the streets.

On Friday 29th January 2021 (I remember the date as it was my husband's seventieth birthday) my husband and I presented at the community mental health team after several phone calls. I was assessed by two workers, and later by a psychiatrist. At first, the mental health team suggested that I should be medicated for the weekend, and reassessed on the Monday, but my husband said that he would be unable to mount a suicide watch for the whole weekend, so the team decided that I should be admitted. I was told that if I didn't comply with advice regarding admission to Hafan y Coed, I could be sectioned. We were met at the mental health care unit by two further workers, and it was concluded that I be accommodated with my agreement.

On arrival on the ward the staff members' first job was to go through and record my belongings, and to inform me of the frequency of monitoring, which was to be every fifteen minutes as I was considered to be at high risk of self-harm. The room was basic, with a chair that was weighted down with sand so it was impossible to throw around. There were built-in shelves on which to put clothing, but no hangers. In the bathroom there were no taps, only press buttons, and the shower was limited to three bursts of water at any one time. The staff, I later discovered, regularly checked everyone's room for litter or anything else that might be used to self-harm.

I spent a lot of time in my room and refused to speak to my husband for around six weeks. I didn't want to speak to him as I believed he no longer wished to be with me. I was anxious about telling people that I was a social worker in case anyone had associated this with negative experiences, so that affected my ability to mix with other patients. In general, everyone behaved well on the ward. This was particularly positive as, due to Covid, activities off the ward had been cancelled. I was, of course, prescribed medication; this was given out along with everyone else's, in the morning and at night. I found that by about 9.30pm I was ready for bed, which is very early for me.

After a discussion with one of the nurses, I started talking to my husband, James. He also started to visit every other day. I was allowed two half-hour periods off the ward which, with permission, I lumped together for James's visit. I was not allowed off site at this time. For James, the visits must have been very difficult – I was convinced that he was seeing someone else. I was also still convinced that James would rip me off and that I would become destitute. I also thought that my pension would not pay out. Staff on the ward contacted James to check these matters with him. The concerns I had about my phone and computer also continued.

In late March, I was seen on one occasion by a different psychiatrist. He was of the view that I could go home, the positives outweighing the negatives in my situation. I rang my husband to inform him of this and to make arrangements for him to collect me. James appeared worried when he came for me – I had apparently told him earlier that day that I was still suicidal. I now know that he contacted the ward to express his surprise that I was being released, given what I had said earlier that day.

My stay at home was short lived – less than a week. This time I was planning a suicide attempt more carefully. The day after I got home (a Thursday) I told my husband I was going for a walk and made several visits to different shops in the area to buy paracetamol. Finding the right time to take the tablets was more problematic. My husband had to go for a Covid booster jab on the Monday, so I decided that was my opportunity. I took more than ninety paracetamols. When James returned home, he quickly realised I had taken something because I was lying on the bed in a very drowsy state, and he called an ambulance.

I was admitted to hospital, where I remained for approximately one week whilst various tests were undertaken. I was seen by mental health professionals and agreed to return to Hafan y Coed on a voluntary basis. Looking back, I find it hard to believe that I thought the suicide attempt would work since I only had a short period alone. I do remember how desperate I felt to take my own life. I was eventually discharged, but I made a third suicide attempt after a few weeks, this time using prescribed medication. I can remember little of that episode, save to say I was once more an inpatient at Hafan y Coed. Although this was only supposed to be a short admission, it actually stretched into two months.

It was during this period that ECT was first suggested by my psychiatrist. I then had a conversation with the ECT team, in an interview room on the ward. I started talking about the desperate situation I was in and how nothing could work. I told the doctor that I was the executor of my husband's will and that would be so complicated to go through, that I could not see how I could possibly cope with it. The doctor must have pictured my husband as being quite poorly. At this point, James walked into the room, looking healthy and confident, and with something of a spring in his step. The doctor told me later how his jaw dropped at this 'miraculous' appearance by a person expected to be on his way out of this world, although I didn't notice anything unusual at the time. This incident confirmed his view that ECT was the right treatment for me.

I must admit that, at first, I was horrified by the suggestion. I had always thought of ECT in terms of an analogy, whereby all the furniture in the doll's house is in the wrong rooms. ECT, as I understood it, is about throwing all the furniture in the air and hoping it lands in the right rooms! After I spoke to staff from the ECT unit, as well as someone with lived experience, I decided to go ahead. After all, nothing else was working!

ECT commenced in November and had a positive impact from the beginning. After the first treatment, I became much less suicidal (although that wore off after another few days). Subsequent treatments made a marked difference, each one leaving me better than before, until it was possible for me to be discharged in early December of 2022. It's a measure of how successful ECT was that my husband had already left for France, in order to celebrate our son-in-law's fortieth birthday. He continued on to Spain and I was able to fly out, on my own, to join him. This would have been unthinkable even a few months earlier. We later drove back to France to celebrate Christmas with our daughter and grandchildren, and then back to the UK to see the New Year in.

This year (2023) I got my life back. I have acted in a play, I spoke at a conference of the Royal College of Psychiatrists and I have volunteered as a mentor for other ECT candidates. I have spent a week teaching social work in Germany and have been able to help our other daughter with work on her new house. As my husband puts it, I have been 'returned to factory settings'.

A Word from James

This has not been an easy journey! Sue went off the rails in 2020, but the seeds of her problems were sown much earlier, when she was pretty much forced out of the work she loved. As an intelligent, talented woman she suddenly found herself filling in her days as a 'lady who lunches' rather than being one of life's movers and shakers. Added to that, during the first Covid lockdown, she was stuck on her own for four months in a fairly large house, unable to socialise, and feeling ill. We talked every day, sometimes twice a day, via FaceTime but I didn't grasp how ill she actually was because she didn't want to worry me. On the plus side, we have wonderful neighbours and friends who checked on her regularly (as best they could, given the Covid restrictions), but Sue is not someone who is happy on her own (unlike me), so this was a difficult period for her.

In the autumn of that year, she began to get some weird ideas. She's never been comfortable with IT, and has always avoided it wherever possible, but this aversion developed into a major fear. I don't know to what extent long Covid played a part, but she was very convincing when she talked about the computer viruses, the dark web and her belief that I was leaving her and stealing all the money. I have to say that this was difficult to handle – I Googled it and discovered that I shouldn't confront the delusions. But how to do that in practice? If I say 'but I'm not leaving you', that's a confrontation, but if I don't say anything that just confirms the delusion. So, this Google advice falls into the category of 'useless'.

The situation at home became untenable. I have a number of business interests and other activities, and to have Sue continually coming in and accusing me of trying to rip her off made it hard to keep on top of everything. At the same time, I was having to pick up more of the minutiae of daily living because Sue was usually spending her days fully dressed, with a bag packed, expecting someone to be coming to the house to evict her. My own mental health was suffering, and I was bending the ears of various friends.

The culmination was on my seventieth birthday. My daughters had chipped in together to send me a delivery of fresh seafood, so I had two live crabs and a live lobster loping around the worktops while Sue was marching around dressed in everything she owned, demanding to know when she was going to be chucked out. Mental health services had promised to phone me back, but the phone kept ringing with people wishing me a 'Happy Birthday!', in several languages, so I wasn't sure if they could get through. Finally, around 2pm, they agreed to see her. Since Sue thought that she was being hoofed out, we had to take all her clothes with us, but we got there in the end, and she was admitted to Hafan y Coed. At last, she was safe – but, of course, all her fears were realised, and she wouldn't speak to me for several weeks.

Her psychiatrist phoned me a couple of days later and went through a list of Sue's delusions in order to check whether any of them were true. At the end, she said 'I don't need to ask about this one, but she thinks she's covered in fur.' In fact, that was the only sane thing Sue had said – it's what she says when she hasn't had her legs waxed for a while. So, there was some hope after all.

10. The Doll's House

Long story short, the next couple of months were eventful, to say the least. But, finally, someone suggested ECT and, despite our initial horror at the prospect, Sue agreed to give it a try. We are now very much converts to ECT: it has given Sue her life back and has given me Sue back. She's still on medication, which sometimes makes her dozy, but, essentially, she's Sue again.

I'm a former professor of marketing, so don't be offended when I say that 'Electro-Convulsive Therapy' is a scary brand name. I suggest calling it 'Control, Alt, Delete.' You'll get better sales, honest! Ironic, I know, as it was a fear of computers and computer viruses which were part of Sue's issues. But we all know that this process is a simple fix for most computer problems, and ECT was the perfect fix for Sue.

11

When Grief Breaks the Brain
Jennifer's Story

11. When Grief Breaks the Brain

1st June 2021

The day I lost my happy life forever.

Prescribed Sertraline over phone. Couldn't tolerate. Sleeping pills too. Terrible.

Mirtazapine 15mg then 30mg – horrible.

Norman and Jennifer are lying to me, they told me I was still on 15mg.

Also on Valium.

Miserable life and no hope for the future. Just drugged for weeks.

All I have to see in future is massive weight gain and the end of my once happy life.

Treated like a docile animal.

This heartbreaking diary entry is my mum's. She wrote this in June 2021, one month before she was admitted to our local psychiatric hospital. She was diagnosed with Catastrophic Breakdown with Psychosis. Her world, and ours, had fallen apart. Again.

To understand my mum's story, I'm going to go back in time to my birth and the circumstances into which I was born. My mum's condition, I firmly believe, is a result of grief; she has had three major bereavements in her life.

My mum is one of ten children, and I was the first grandchild in the family, born in early 1978. My birth should have been a happy time, but it wasn't.

My mum and dad met at school in their teens and fell in love. They dated and spent the late seventies enjoying their romance, going to music concerts, eating nice dinners in restaurants and spending time with family. My dad was a talented footballer and was signed by Celtic Football Club when he was just seventeen – he was destined for great things in the sporting world. Their future looked shiny and happy. When they were both just twenty, they discovered that Mum was pregnant. Mum tells me she was terrified: what would her parents say? They weren't married and I was planned – just not yet, maybe a few years down the line. But, according to my mum, my dad was over the moon with excitement, told her not to worry and was with her when she told her parents. He was the strong one and told my grandparents that he loved their daughter, he loved me and they were going to be married. Thankfully, my grandparents were delighted for them, and the next few months centred on planning for the wedding and then planning for my arrival. Sadly, my father never got to meet me because he collapsed on the pitch, was taken into hospital and died three days later. He died on the 5th December 1977, and I was born on 6th January 1978. It was acute leukaemia, not previously detected, and resulted in his sudden, shocking death.

My mum and I lived with my grandparents until I was nearly five years old, and all I remember is a happy and enchanting childhood. I loved the buzz of the busy house, full of people, and, being the baby, was spoiled by all of the family, all of the time! Looking back, I can't believe how strong my mum was. I know, from my grandparents and my aunties and uncles, that she was utterly and profoundly devastated. Of course, she struggled badly in those early months. But she had a focus in me, she had to be strong for me. And strong she was. In fact, all through my life, until that time in 2021, she had been a powerhouse of a woman. She's petite and very slim built – but my goodness, is she a force of nature! It was Mum who did all the DIY around the house. If we were unwell, she'd consult her medical books and knew exactly what to do. If anybody upset us kids or treated us badly, the lioness in her would come out, and she was never short of conversation (a trait that seems to be shared in the family).

Again, looking back, I am full of admiration as to how she coped with such tragedy at such a young age, but my dad's death wasn't her first experience of grief. Five years before his death, when she was only fifteen, her ten-year-old sister, Roseann, was hit by a car and killed instantly. My family had therefore already been through the death of a young person in sudden, tragic circumstances.

11. When Grief Breaks the Brain

I don't know how they coped with both of these events, but people do and, as the old cliché goes, life goes on.

Mum remarried years later and was very happy. She and my new dad went on to have two more children: my sister, Gillian, and then my brother, Peter. As the three of us grew up, we had a happy childhood and a normal life. Time passed, I went to university then started my career, moved out of home. Mum and dad split up after twenty-three years of marriage, and years after that she remarried again, to Norman, her husband now. Life was normal.

But in March 2020, the third bereavement in my mum's life devastated her, and all of us. My thirty-three-year-old brother Peter died suddenly. The Covid-19 lockdown was announced by the UK government three days later. We were one of the first families to experience the unprecedented times of trying to grieve and bury a loved one whilst not being allowed to be together. Only Mum, Dad, Gillian, and I were allowed at the funeral service (my partner and Norman had to stand outside the building). We couldn't go for a cup of tea after the service, we couldn't embrace each other, and we couldn't grieve together. Like many families, we accepted this and tried to deal with Peter's death in our own way. Mum, again, seemed strong and resilient, but hindsight is a wonderful thing and, looking back, I wish I could have seen the signs that she wasn't coping, wasn't dealing with it. Having studied sociology at university, I know all too well how important rituals are to our society; as human beings, we need these societal rituals to help us deal with loss. Consequently, when you're isolated and alone, what does that do to the mind? Whilst the previous two bereavements in my mum's life were equally as catastrophic, she had people around her, people to talk with, cry with, laugh with, but due to the Covid restrictions after Peter's death, she had none of this, all of which is so important for the grieving process.

All these tragic experiences lead me to the diary entry quoted above. She shared it with me three years after she wrote it; she found it inside a notebook.

About a year after Peter's death, in the months leading to her breakdown, Mum's mood became really low. I remember Gillian and I visiting her in her garden (which was allowed by then) on Mother's Day. Mum would normally have been running around the garden with Gillian's two young boys, laughing and having a great time because all they had known until then was their fun grandma. But by this time, she was different. She was sad, withdrawn, unable to smile, let alone laugh or play with her grandkids. She was very honest with us and told us that she'd been feeling very down and was struggling to sleep. She went to her GP, described her symptoms and was prescribed antidepressants – something which she had never taken before, and something which she will now admit she didn't want to take at the time. She called me that night to say she'd read about them and tossed them in the bin. Again, looking back, I just thought that's Mum, headstrong as usual; she will come through this herself, as she always had done when dealing with death. But not this time.

Things deteriorated rapidly over those summer months. She became so depressed that she and Norman reached out to the local mental health team, and she was referred to the crisis team who came out to talk to her, advise her on ways to help her to sleep and offer support going forward. This went on for several weeks, but she continued to get worse.

I remember vividly the day she went into full psychosis, although I didn't know it then. They were having a summer house built in their garden, and whilst Norman was outside with the builders, she told me she was terrified that they couldn't afford this and that they were on the brink of bankruptcy. I was shocked and, at the time, I believed her. None of this was true. What we know now is that her psychosis presented in two forms of delusions: firstly, that she was going to lose her house and that she was financially destitute and secondly, that she was going to become grossly overweight. By this time, she weighed around six and a half stone. I must point out here that, even though mental ill health is devastating, I have found moments of real humour and levity (I'm only able to laugh now years later, but some of the things she said were actually really funny, as I'll highlight in anecdotes throughout this chapter).

The final straw (which was also funny, looking back on it now) was the day she insisted on making an evening meal for herself and Norman which involved enough chicken to feed more than ten people, an entire kilo of potatoes, and an excessive amount of turnips because she believed she needed to eat and eat and eat. Norman says it was the amount of turnips that finally tipped him over the edge. The mental health team were called as what Mum was saying didn't make sense, she couldn't be calmed down, and all her anxieties – namely, money worries and weight gain – were becoming completely irrational and all-consuming. She was also becoming very anxious that she was going to get into bother with the mental health team because she hadn't completed their exercise books – this wasn't a stipulation from the team, simply a way to help her focus, but she became fixated that she must fill in this workbook. Norman and I noticed that she couldn't write one single line, no matter how she tried to express her feelings. This was another huge red flag to me. Mum had always been very clever and had a flair for writing and expressing herself. Watching her struggle to compose a sentence or even write down a few words, we knew this was bad and something was really wrong with her mind.

On the 16th July 2021, the crisis team came to the house and calmly suggested to Norman and me that Mum may need to be admitted into hospital. We agreed, and together we all tried to explain to her that accepting this, and going in voluntarily, would be best all round. She was like a little frightened rabbit, and I'll never forget the fear in her eyes that day. Sadly, but fortunately, she agreed, and I drove them to the hospital in my car. We drove there in silence.

Taking your mother into a psychiatric ward, seeing her being assessed and continuing to express her delusions to the doctor was nothing short of heartbreaking. No matter how many times we told her she was not in any financial trouble, and that actually she was seriously underweight, she just couldn't accept it and argued that we were wrong and she was right. But the most heartbreaking thing was leaving her there and not knowing when or how she could be fixed.

Again, due to ongoing Covid restrictions, only two people were permitted onto the ward to visit, so Norman and I agreed a timetable: one of us would go after lunch and one of us would go after dinner. The staff on the ward were amazing and reassured us that, in most cases, with the right medication, most patients will recover. It's all about getting the mood lifted and then the psychosis will begin to diminish and recovery will follow. We put our faith in the experts and the process, and Mum was trialled on the first set of medication.

I understand that, with any medication, it takes time, but over the course of the entire four months that Mum was in hospital we all began to recognise (staff included) that the medication was just not working, and Mum was continuing to decline in front of us. My strong mother had become a mental patient in a mental ward, shuffling up and down a corridor thousands of times a day, not wearing any shoes, and telling us she was too scared to change clothes because she was frightened of getting dressed. To lighten this memory, as it does get very dark, I can recall a very funny moment. I arrived on the ward, and Mum came rushing towards me with a frightened look on her face. She said 'I'm going to be 19 stone tomorrow, so you'll have to bring in your clothes as mine won't fit anymore.' Now, I might not be six and a half stone like her, but I was only a size 12! I laughed and told her she was a cheeky lady, and I wasn't that big! But even this memory, whilst comical, is sad, because she just didn't get my joke. She couldn't see humour, couldn't read or express emotion, and just continued to reiterate the delusions that were in her head. It was so sad, and, two months into her hospital admission, I began to feel hopeless.

Over the months that followed, Mum continued to decline; she was convinced the staff hated her and believed that the cars parked outside the hospital had been deliberately parked there by the hospital authorities to let her know they were watching her. Even her face had changed. Every day we visited, she met us with the same worried frown, a frown that I've never seen before; she looked like she was haunted by some awful, dark demon inside her. Smiling was not an option. No matter how often we tried to tell her stories which would always in the past have initiated a smile or a laugh, especially when it was about her two little grandsons, whom she adored, nothing broke through the barrier. That frightened little rabbit was all that was there now.

As a family, we were in constant discussion about what else could be done for Mum, what other medication combinations might be tried next. Would the psychiatrist on the ward try something different because we all knew that, up until now, nothing was working? After various discussions with the medical team, one day the consultant psychiatrist called me at home to update me on Mum's health and their proposed clinical decision. They were going to try electroconvulsive therapy (ECT). The doctor explained that she hadn't come to this decision lightly, and ECT is often a last resort, especially when so many different antidepressants have not worked. I listened as she explained the procedure and all that was involved. Of course, my first reaction (and everyone else who I subsequently told) was 'do they still do that?!' and of course, everyone comments (as did I) on the only cultural reference we know relating to electric shock therapy: the portrayal in the film *One*

Flew Over the Cuckoo's Nest. But the doctor was excellent in laying out the way the procedure is administered today: if she was medically well and fit enough to have the ECT, Mum would be given a general anaesthetic and a muscle relaxant, and a very small seizure would be induced. The whole process takes around 30 minutes, and she'd be back on the ward within a few hours. She would have two treatments a week, one on a Tuesday and one on a Friday, and the typical course would be twelve treatments, but she might not even need them all.

Rather than be terrified or buy into the idea that this was a horrifying treatment, I decided to research the subject as much as I could and spent a long time googling the term, reading various medical journals, listening to podcasts, and, in general, educating myself on how it works in 2021 and crucially, what the outcome might be. What I discovered filled me with hope. Of course, there are side effects, and I was concerned about the risk of Mum suffering memory loss, but everything I read pointed out that it was mostly short-term memory loss which often improves when the course of treatment stops. I reasoned with myself that if she lost any short-term memories, it would only be of the frightening, dark world that she was now living in anyway. So, as a family, we put our faith in the process, and in the clinical team, who were brilliant at providing us with all the information we needed and answered all our questions candidly and clearly.

After passing all the health checks, Mum went in for her first session at 10am on a Tuesday morning in October. Norman and I didn't do our alternate visiting that day; we both went together for the lunchtime visit, full of excitement and fully believing that we would see her completely back to herself as soon as we walked through the secure doors. That hope was swiftly kicked away when she came towards us looking and sounding exactly as she had the day before. We were gutted. However, I really want to emphasise this to whoever might read this and be going through

11. When Grief Breaks the Brain

the exact same thing right now: please don't give up or worry if it doesn't work straight away. Of course, I can only speak for my mother's case, but it did work. The next few weeks were terrible: she had two sessions a week and there appeared to be absolutely no change in her whatsoever. Then, on the fourth week, with the seventh ECT session, we saw a slight glimmer of hope. Mum was engaging more in conversation and she wasn't avoiding the nursing staff – in fact she was having conversations with them, she was asking us about us and her grandchildren, and there was a slight, very slight, hint of a smile at one point.

That Friday, everything changed. After her eighth ECT session, she came walking towards me with a big smile on her face, her hair freshly washed and wearing a lovely scarf to accessorise her outfit. She even asked for her make up bag and hair straighteners! We were allowed to leave the hospital for a coffee and, whilst sitting in a coffee shop, with Mum doing all the chatting, she commented to me 'Those lovely nurses said a really sweet thing to me earlier ... they told me I had a lovely smile, and that it was so good to see it. My goodness, I must have been a right little misery guts if they haven't even seen me smile!' That's when I knew I had my mum back.

--

This should have been the happy ending to a terrible time in all our lives. However, mental illness doesn't work like that, and nor does grief. Mum was back, for almost a year actually, but then she wasn't. Unsurprisingly, her decline happened in March, the anniversary of Peter's death. We could all see it, Mum could even see it too, but again, it consumed her. She was lethargic, sad, disinterested in life, her appearance, and all of us. This time, thankfully there were no signs of psychosis, but the vibrant happy person was gone once again, and nothing could make her smile any more.

I was swept back into a world of despair; we all were. So, I decided to try a new tactic: cold water therapy. If she wasn't in psychosis, maybe she didn't need to be readmitted to hospital. Maybe she just needed pulling out of this new depressive state, and cold water therapy had become the 'new thing' for helping with mental health. We're lucky in that we live near one of Scotland's most beautiful lochs, and the temperature in the loch is freezing! Perfect. I set about buying all the equipment we would need: neoprene socks and gloves, a large dry robe each, for drying and changing afterwards, and woolly hats for our heads – we were going in with just our swimsuits on! Mum was not up for this at all, but somehow I managed to coax her into the car; during the twenty-minute journey to the loch, she muttered about how she did not want to do this, it would not help and she just wanted to go home and lie on the couch. I did my best to jolly her along and tried to change the subject. I fully believed that this was an alternative to ECT, and it would work in almost the same way; the cold water would 'shock' her into feeling better. When we were in the water, I sometimes saw little glimmers of a positive reaction from her, but then the frown would return and she'd say she wanted to get out. Sadly, it didn't work. She was so thin that the worst part was getting out and getting dried off. She was shaking uncontrollably with the cold, and at one point I thought I might have caused her to become hypothermic. We eventually gave up.

Once more, we were back with the mental health team advising us on the best form of treatment, and, once again, Mum was on her way to the hospital. This time, it was specifically for ECT treatment. No more trying her on another form of medication; the clinical team agreed that ECT had worked the last time, so let's try again. Mum was only in hospital for the two days each week that she received the treatment and was allowed home for the rest of the week. This appeased her to some extent, but not a lot. She was terrified again, and not happy with us for agreeing to send her back in there.

Her second course of ECT took place pretty much one year after she was admitted the first time, and once again it didn't seem to work straight away. I knew that session eight was the winner last year so held my nerve until we reached that number this time. Sessions eight, nine, ten, and eleven all came and went, and she was still utterly depressed. The hopelessness I felt this time was palpable. What if this was it? What if this was going to be her life now? The medication hadn't worked, ECT had worked last year but now seemed to have no impact on her mood. But then, incredibly, the very last session, the twelfth, was the winner this time. I couldn't believe it, but once again, she came walking towards us and something in her had changed. She was back and she was smiling.

I'm lucky that, at the point that I write this, there is a happy ending. Mum is now really well; it's been two years since her last ECT, and we're all hoping she'll never need it again. The anniversary of losing Peter comes around every year, but our feelings of loss and grief are not an annual thing; it's a daily thing and his loss is something we will never get over, just live with. And that's what Mum has been doing: living.

As a family we put our faith in the medical teams who looked after Mum, and for them we are truly grateful. But that first year, Mum was in the hospital for four months, being tried on various medication combinations, before she was given ECT; it was a last resort. The second year she was better at the end of just six weeks. In my opinion, based purely on my mum's case, I wonder why ECT is always considered a last resort? Perhaps if it had been considered earlier, her broken brain would have been 'fixed' sooner and she would not have endured those long torturous months, perpetually terrified in a hospital ward? But, once again, irrespective of when she received what I consider to be a lifesaving treatment, she is one of the lucky ones, and she's still smiling today.

12

The Making of *Waves of Hope*

The creation of this book didn't follow a pre-planned path. Working as a consultant psychiatrist in an ECT clinic for more than twenty years, I have aimed to inform the public about the effectiveness of this treatment. I wanted to share some of the dramatic recoveries of very ill patients that I have witnessed, the transformations of people from the depths of psychosis, the agony of depression or stupor to complete recovery. No other treatment in psychiatry can match some of these outcomes in terms of the speed or magnitude of the changes; this is probably on par with some surgical outcomes in terms of life-restoring effects. Despite that, most people still see ECT as a barbaric treatment that has no place in modern psychiatry, perhaps something to be ashamed of. Even some medical colleagues look astounded when they hear what I do in the hospital.

During the first Covid-19 lockdown, I launched a book called *Shocked* which narrated the stories of patients receiving ECT in my clinic. It attracted some interest in ECT circles, and among

12. The Making of *Waves of Hope*

a number of patients and their relatives. Colleagues started contacting me for advice and feedback. But this book was never going to change public perceptions. Nor were scientific papers going to make a difference. I reasoned that stories narrated by patients themselves, in their own words, would be seen as more credible, and would feel more powerful.

Gradually, the idea emerged of setting up a team of patients who have had ECT and relatives who have looked after their loved ones during this treatment. I started talking about this with people who had written blogs, with those who contacted me by email for advice or who were active on Twitter (now X), and with some of my patients. Initially, it looked only to be an aspirational project, with close to zero chance of success, like some of the other projects that I had started and abandoned over the years. What would motivate someone to disclose, publicly, such a traumatic experience, and to admit that they had undergone what is seen as a stigmatising treatment? Very few people have spoken publicly about it – or, at least, I couldn't find many.

By the end of 2022, nine people had expressed an interest in the project and, to my surprise, they didn't need to be persuaded to publish their stories. In February 2023 we had our first group Zoom meeting to discuss the idea of writing a book. The most common questions raised then, and discussed again at subsequent meetings, were 'who is this book for?' and, related to that, 'what should be the style?' I had my own views, but so did everyone else, and so we kept talking about the style and the target audience. Was it going to be for mental health professionals, to educate them about the feelings and problems experienced by patients, the things that they wouldn't tell you but that you should be aware of? Was it to educate the public about ECT, to reduce the stigma and the misinformation? Should the style be informative and factual, or more personal and emotional: to read more like a novel, so that it is more accessible for members of the public? Or should it be aimed at patients, and their relatives, who are considering this treatment, to provide them with the information they need, delivered by other patients, so that they are more likely to trust the procedure?

For the first meeting, I invited only a few people who I thought could lead on these discussions, but by the second meeting, a month later, all prospective authors were invited. Everybody began contributing suggestions on the writing of the stories, on what could make a good read. One person suggested that to make a story gripping, you should give more information about yourself: what your emotions were at the time, what it felt like to be depressed or psychotic. Others commented that we should lift the stigma that surrounds ECT by showing that this can happen to anybody – even being detained under the Mental Health Act can happen to people who are well educated and who hold responsible jobs.

At the next meeting, several people joined for the first time and hadn't yet met the others, so we went through the standard introductions. Instead of just stating their name and background, the accounts became unexpectedly long: people were already starting to narrate their stories and were happy to share them with like-minded people. It was as if they needed to pour out facts that had been untold for years. Everybody had a unique story, full of emotions and full of messages for the public. There were messages for me, too, as I began realising that there can be much more beneath what I usually discuss with my patients.

I had estimated that the chances of finding a publisher were close to zero and had resigned myself to self-publishing. But we all felt that we should at least try a few publishers. In July 2023, I approached the Royal College of Psychiatrists, which publishes books in collaboration with Cambridge University Press. To my surprise and delight, we were invited to submit a book proposal. This demonstrated a strong dedication to patients who benefit from this treatment and showed courage in addressing a contentious subject. I felt proud to be part of this college.

This offer suddenly made everything real and urgent, and I realised, with some anxiety, that work had to start immediately – and, worryingly, that we might not get enough good stories. Until that point, I had seen short drafts from three or four people, mostly written in a rather factual style. None of them, so far, was good enough for a book, and we were miles away from having a product that would attract interest.

Another Zoom meeting followed, aimed at discussing how to write a good account. It was the detail that mattered, we argued, what you were thinking and feeling at the time: tell us about the despair, the pain you felt. Think how your story could provoke a tear, or a smile. Keep the reader intrigued, wanting to find out what happens at the end. As we started talking about describing feelings, another problem became obvious: this was a stressful experience for people who had already suffered a breakdown and gone through horrible times. What if somebody gets traumatised by the experience, or even suffers a relapse of their illness? Should people get support, and, if so, who will provide this support? Several of the authors had already delivered support work in different settings for people going through difficult times. They offered to support anybody who felt stressed. I wondered whether the care that people were already showing each other during these meetings could be the right type of help they needed, as we were now looking a bit like a community. It was indeed an emotional journey. One person did drop out, admitting that they could not look through the diaries they had written at the time as the memories were too painful. However, towards the end, the remaining authors were pleased that they had done it. Here are some of the accounts they shared:

> Writing my story, and sharing it with others, has made me more confident and I feel able to come to terms with what I have

experienced over almost two decades. It has helped me process what has happened to me.

This was the first time I had looked at my experiences in their entirety. I have previously drawn upon and shared parts of my story that I felt to be relevant. To sit down with my recollections, medical notes and diaries I had written at the time was both emotional and at the same time cathartic. I feel that I have accepted and acknowledged the good and the bad about my experience and myself.

Writing my story was highly emotional and mentally draining, in part because I decided to check back on my online GP medical records to be sure of the dates I was including. The relief of that stress has come from the support and encouragement I received for my writing from the friends and my (now adult) kids who feature in the chapter.

Several of our authors went through difficult times during the two or three years of this project (reassuringly, not as a result of writing their stories), and I was impressed by their commitment, as they stayed in touch throughout, one even emailing during a hospital admission.

At the author meetings, people continued opening up, talking at length about their feelings in a way they hadn't expressed in their stories until that point. Quite often, I would stare at the attendees on the computer screen, touched by their accounts, and say 'This is such a powerful statement, write down in your story what you just said.' And people did open up and start describing their emotions.

Still, I was worried about the outcome. After all, none of the contributors was a professional writer, and even if some of them had a talent for writing, why should we expect that everybody would produce a great story? Then, one day, the following text appeared on my computer screen as the start of a story: 'I am thirty-one weeks pregnant with my first child. It is five o'clock in the morning and I awake to find my bed soaking wet. Knowing that urinary incontinence is not unusual in the later stages of

12. The Making of *Waves of Hope*

pregnancy, at first, I think I must have wet the bed. But there is a lot of liquid, and it keeps coming.' I moved closer to the screen, feeling goosebumps on my skin, anticipating the drama that will follow a premature birth, and kept on reading. The story continued building up to some dramatic events. I knew we would have a book! OK, we needed another ten stories like that.

And the stories started coming, full of drama and emotions. People who had sent me factual accounts before had completely rewritten their stories. Poems started appearing, extracts from diaries written at the time and probably not seen by anyone else; there were tears, and there was humour too. Desperation alternated with elation. There was no need to worry that the stories would be too similar, such as 'woman gets depressed, has ECT and gets well'. None of that; every story had something unique and was written in its author's own style.

The publisher's initial reviews of the book outline were positive. They had seen only the first parts of two stories and, doubtful that everyone would be able to match the style, suggested that we employ a professional writer to interview the participants. This had been my plan too. But our authors disagreed: 'our voices should be heard and not altered' was the majority response. And so, it was decided that, among us, we would provide structural editorial advice and proofreading, that we would recommend what to change, what to add or delete, and we would encourage people to remember more details here and there, but we would not change the style or the choice of words. The authenticity of each story would be kept. My role suddenly became a lot easier: I would not have to rewrite anything. I engaged Jennifer to provide developmental editing and together we reviewed the stories, going through four or five iterations on some occasions. We started meeting with each author separately, suggesting ways to improve their story without trying to change their style. My ECT clinic nurse, Olivia, helped with more editing and advice on getting the NHS issues right. Ruth proved to be a high-quality proof-reader when I asked her to check one of the stories, so I was delighted when she agreed to edit and proof-read all of them. One day Ruth (yes, the same Ruth) sent us an illustration for her story that had been drawn by Milton at her request. The clarity of the message in the artwork was obvious, so we decided we wanted an illustration for each chapter. Like the stories, some of these drawings also underwent several rounds of editing, until they satisfied the authors' imagination, with Milton remaining accommodating and patient.

The reviewers of the book advised that we should also include stories that do not have positive outcomes and those that discuss side effects, especially memory problems. This was not difficult, as not all stories had great outcomes and most journeys were far from smooth. Admittedly, the stories in this book tend to be more positive than what happens to the average person receiving ECT, and I should remind readers of the expected statistics listed in the Introduction, of just over 40 per cent of depressed patients in the UK achieving remission, while two-thirds being rated as 'much improved' or 'very much improved'. The authors in this book had suffered with severe depression or mania, and all had experienced psychotic features at least at some point. These clinical pictures are more likely to respond well to ECT. However, when our authors started describing the details of side effects and other problems, there was no paucity of negative accounts, to the point that I wondered whether this reflected the average adverse experiences. These accounts were left as they were written, even if uncomfortable for prospective candidates for ECT. We didn't want to preach in favour of ECT, we only needed to give real accounts of what happens.

I will finish with an expression of my gratitude and admiration for what our authors have achieved here, and what they went through for the sake of lifting the stigma that surrounds this treatment.

George Kirov, October 2024

For EU product safety concerns, contact us at Calle de José Abascal, 56–1°, 28003 Madrid, Spain or eugpsr@cambridge.org.

www.ingramcontent.com/pod-product-compliance
Ingram Content Group UK Ltd.
Pitfield, Milton Keynes, MK11 3LW, UK
UKHW022021170226
468134UK00021B/510